Master Principles of Evangelism

Delos Miles

BROADMAN PRESS

Nashville, Tennessee

To
Nada
my beloved wife
and amanuensis

Contents

Preface

Matthew's Gospel quotes Jesus as saying, "A disciple is not above his teacher, nor a servant above his master; it is enough for the disciple to be like his teacher, and the servant like his master" (Matt. 10: 24-25). Apply that saying to evangelism.

What was our Master model like in his evangelism? What major principles of evangelism may we learn from the perfect Teacher?

Jesus was the evangelist par excellence. He was the evangelist without a peer. He was the master disciple winner. He knew what was in persons. If we wish to learn how to win individuals, let us study his ways with them; not to slavishly imitate his methods, but to discern the great principles which guided his work with the unreconciled. Methods change from generation to generation and from place to place. All one has to do to see that is to study a little church history. But principles seldom change.

At least one writer thinks there "has been an extreme overemphasis on techniques and methods without explaining the principles."[1] While I doubt there has been an extreme overemphasis, I do believe these two aspects of evangelism should be balanced and that the techniques and methods should grow out of the principles.

What I should like to do in this volume is to make an inquiry into some principles of evangelism according to Christ. Jesus had no stereotyped methods. He dealt with no two cases exactly the same way.

Chapter 1 is an introduction to the eight master principles. The sentences immediately below the title of each chapter are intended to summarize the content and thrust of the respective chapters. I have included a Scripture lesson from both the Old and New Testaments for each chapter. These principles are based solidly on the Bible. Those who read the Scripture lessons prior to reading the respective chapters may get more mileage out of the book. I hope what I wrote will be read in the light of an open Bible.

Mark Twain once quipped: "Adam was the only man who, when he said a good thing, knew that nobody had said it before him." If you should find any good things in the pages which follow, I know they are not good because they are new. My hope is that they are good because they are true. The notes on each chapter are included in order to give proper credit to my sources and to point the reader beyond this book.

Portions of chapters 2 to 5 were shared in embryo form as a lecture at Golden Gate Baptist Theological Seminary in 1975. That particular lecture was published in a 1976 supplement of *Home Missions* magazine.[2] Riverland Hills Baptist Church in Columbia, South Carolina, was gracious enough to let me use them in 1980 as a guinea pig for much of the material in its present form. I have been testing these principles in churches, associations, evangelism conferences, college campuses, and seminary classrooms in America during the past decade. Particularly have I found them useful in the Lay Evangelism Schools which I have conducted.

J. Wilbur Chapman, a noted Presbyterian evangelist, in the first stanza of his hymn, "One Day," gives voice to what my heart feels about these master principles of evangelism:

> One day when heaven was filled with his praises,
> One day when sin was black as could be,
> Jesus came forth to be born of a virgin,
> Dwelt among men, my example is he![3]

If we major on anything in our evangelism, let it be the imitation of Christ. Finally, if what follows does not seem relevant to you, remember the advice of Von Hugel: "We ought never to snort at what does not now help us, but may help others."

Notes

1. George R. Jaffray, Jr., *Explosive Evangelism* (MacDill AFB, Fla.: Tyndale Bible Society, 1972), p. 41.

2. See my article, "Jesus, Master Evangelist," *Home Missions,* Vol. 47, No. 4, April, 1976, pp. 24e-24h.

3. J. Wilbur Chapman, "One Day," *Baptist Hymnal,* 1975, No. 127. Copyright 1910 by C. H. Marsh. Copyright Renewed 1938 (extended) by Chas. H. Marsh. Assigned to The Rodeheaver Co. Used by permission.

1
Fishers of People

Theme: One learns how to fish for people by following Jesus
Scripture Lesson: Jonah 1:17; Mark 1:16-20

Introduction

The cross has become the most widely used symbol for Christianity. And rightly so because "without the shedding of blood there is no forgiveness of sins" (Heb. 9:22). Moreover, on the cross God showed his love for us in that "while we were yet sinners Christ died for us" (Rom. 5:8).

But the cross has not always been the most widely used symbol for the Christian faith. Back in the early centuries of the church, when Christians were persecuted and martyred for their faith, the fish was the symbol which Christians used. The symbol of the fish and the word *ichthus* (the Greek word for fish) became a secret symbol and password for Christians who were forbidden to openly practice their faith.

The second half of this century has seen a widespread return to the symbol of the fish and to the word *ichthus*. However, it all began when Jesus said to certain fishermen: "Follow me and I will make you become fishers of men" (Mark 1:17).

Meaning

What did Jesus mean by those words? The invitation was issued to those who had been fishing for a living. They had been catching fish; now they would catch people! The parallel passage to Mark 1:17 in Luke 5:10 brings this out more clearly: "Do not be afraid; henceforth you will be catching men."

The word which Luke used for "catching" comes from the Greek root *zogreo*, which literally means to take alive or to capture for life. Charles G. Trumbull, a prominent leader in the Sunday School movement in America, wrote a book which takes its title from the word *zogreo: Taking Men Alive.* It is Trumbull's contention that fishing for people is taking people alive and capturing them for life.

Trumbull points out that the word *zogreo* is used only twice in the entire New Testament. Luke 5:10 uses the word to describe the work of the disciples. However, 2 Timothy 2:26 uses the word to describe the work of the devil. Hence, both the disciples and the devil are in the business of capturing persons![1]

The devil takes people alive to do his will, to do evil. The disciples take people alive to do God's will, to do good. One thing is sure. If we Christians don't catch persons, the devil will. The devil and his crowd are aggressive in fishing for people. Christians must be more aggressive.

Mode

Now, some of you may be thinking that if fishing for people means catching them and capturing them for life that they may be hurt or used in the process. You may associate catching with a hook and, therefore, with pain and manipulation. Arthur G. McPhee in his book, *Friendship Evangelism,* makes a contrast between net fishing and hook (or angling) fishing. Hook fishing is usually a solo effort while net fishing is usually an enterprise of partners. Hook fishing depends upon trickery and violence, while net fishing is a much more natural method. The hook fisherman usually fishes for sport, while the net fisherman usually fishes for a living. The hook fisherman is more interested in the catching, while the net fisherman is also deeply concerned with the keeping.[2]

Commercial fishing in the first century, as in the twentieth century, was best done with nets. I know some Christians use a fishhook today to signify that they are fishers of people. A more appropriate symbol, however, would be that of a net. We don't hurt persons when we catch them for Christ. On the contrary, we help them. We rescue them. We save them from sin, Satan, death, the grave, and hell. We enable them to escape the terrible wrath of God.

There is one other aspect to fishing with a net which we often overlook. We can catch more fish with a net than we can with a hook. Jesus wants us to catch lots of fish. If it is good to catch one member of a family for Christ, it is even better to catch a whole family for Christ. Fish are caught best in schools. By the same token, persons are caught best in their natural affinity groups such as family, friends, and business associates.

Process

Naturally, one doesn't become an expert fisher of persons instantaneously. Jesus said: "Follow me and I will make you become fishers of men." Fishers of people are *made*. A process of growth is involved.

This does not mean that a brand new Christian cannot fish for people. Immediately after the Gerasene demoniac was healed, Jesus said to him: "Go home to your friends, and tell them how much the Lord has done for you" (Mark 5:19). Furthermore, when the woman of Samaria met Jesus at Jacob's well, she left her water jar and ran back to the city to tell people what had happened. "Many Samaritans from that city believed in him because of the woman's testimony" (John 4:39). We know also from John's Gospel that the first thing Andrew did after he had found Jesus was to go and bring his brother, Simon, to Jesus (see John 1:40-42).

Now, we are beginning to discover that a brand new disciple normally has more contacts and relationships with more lost persons than does one who has been a Christian for several or more years. If we are wise, we shall do everything possible to enable our new converts to fish for people in their natural webs of kinship, friendship, and business associations.

Therefore, while it is true that expert fishers of people are made rather than born, it is also accurate to say that one begins to be made into a fisher of people when he is born into the kingdom of God. The new birth is the genesis of the lifelong process whereby we begin to become fishers of people.

Model

Ultimately, we can learn how to fish for people only by actually fishing for them. Perhaps you have heard the parable of the geese who said they wanted to fly. The geese ate chicken feed six days. On the seventh day a big gander would call them together and talk about flying. Every week they talked about flying. They even concluded the meeting with a song entitled "I'll Fly Away." Then, they went back and repeated the process!

We can't learn how to fish for people just by talking about it or by listening to someone else talk about it—any more than we can learn how to fly an airplane without flying one or learn how to swim without getting into the water.

Jesus gave us an important clue about how to learn to become a fisher of people in his words, "Follow me." Jesus is the Master Fisherman, the fisher of people without a peer.

Indeed, Jesus is the only perfect model Fisherman who ever fished for people. If we would learn how to perfect our skills as fishers of people, let us enroll in the school of Christ. Let us study how Jesus dealt with persons and, with the aid of the Holy Spirit, seek to imitate his example.

Conclusion

Our Scripture lesson from Jonah and Mark offers an interesting contrast. Jonah tells of a fish who caught a man. Mark tells of fishermen who are to catch people. Nevertheless, the two stories are not that far apart. God wanted Jonah to go to Ninevah and fish for people. When Jonah refused, rebelled, and sought to escape, God caused one of his creatures to catch him and deliver him to Ninevah. There was no escape for Jonah.

Jesus intends for you and me to become fishers of people. We may, like Jonah, refuse, rebel, and seek to escape. The only safe course for us, however, is to follow Jesus: "Follow me, and I will make you become fishers of men."

Notes

1. Charles G. Trumbull, *Taking Men Alive* (London: The Religious Tract Society, n.d.), p. 34.

2. Arthur G. McPhee, *Friendship Evangelism* (Grand Rapids, Michigan: Zondervan, 1978), pp. 44-49.

2
Dignity

Theme: Jesus revealed a profound respect for human personality
Scripture Lesson: Genesis 1:26-27; John 4:4-42

Introduction

The first and most important principle of evangelism according to Christ may be respect for personality. Or, if you want it in one word, dignity.

Jesus revealed a profound respect for every person with whom he dealt. And, according to Leighton Ford in *The Christian Persuader,* Christ dealt with at least thirty-five persons face-to-face in the four Gospels.[1]

The Example of Nicodemus

If you will examine these cases, person by person, you will see this principle of respect for personality operating from one end of the social spectrum to the other. Take for example Nicodemus, a wealthy and powerful member of the Sanhedrin. L. R. Scarborough insists that Nicodemus was a rabbi. Some Virginians would call him a blue-blooded intellectual.

If we were to take a justice of the United States Supreme Court, a bishop of the church, and a university professor with his Ph.D. degree and put all three of these men together in one man, we would have an idea of the kind of person Nicodemus was. He was one of the most influential men of his day. In spite of the fact that for some reason he came to Jesus by night, Jesus treated Nicodemus with the same respect and courtesy which he showed to all other people. Jesus did not berate Nicodemus. Jesus neither put Nicodemus down nor set him up on a pedestal.

The Example of a Samaritan Woman

Now, go to the opposite end of the social spectrum and see how Jesus dealt with the woman of Samaria (John 4). If you are ever going to see the principle of dignity, you will surely see it here.

This woman had several strikes against her. To begin with, the fact that she was a woman was against her. That may be hard for us to understand in this day of women's liberation.

Nevertheless, women in the days of Jesus had very low status, even among the Jews in spite of their high concept of one, holy God. Jewish men could do with women pretty much as they pleased so long as they obeyed the law. There was one school of thought which taught that a husband could divorce his wife for something about as minor as burning the morning toast. But the woman could not divorce her husband for the same reason.

Women among the Jews were almost like property which men owned. Every morning when the devout Jewish male arose and said his prayers, he thanked God that he was not born an uncircumcised Gentile or a woman. Women were primarily important because they could bear male children.

This attitude still prevails among some of the Arabs of the Middle East today. Just a few years ago, King Hussein of Jordan divorced his wife ostensibly because she could not bear him a son. Whether that was the real reason or not, the king was able to do it.

Some of the Gnostic heretics went so far as to teach that unless a woman became a male, she could not enter the kingdom of heaven. The Gnostic gospel of Thomas (Logion 114) reads: "Simon Peter said to them (the risen Jesus and his disciples): Let Mary go out from among us, because women are not worthy of life. Jesus said: See, I shall lead her, so that I will make her male, that she too may become a living spirit, resembling you males. For every woman who makes herself male will enter the Kingdom of Heaven."[2]

Jesus, unlike the Gnostics and some of his own kinsmen, shattered all such false stereotypes of women. This truth is caught for us in John 4:27 when we are told that his disciples "marveled that he was talking with a woman.'' They did not marvel that he was talking with a Samaritan or a prostitute, but with a woman. It was customary for a rabbi not to talk with a woman in public. Jesus was considered to be a rabbi; yet, contrary to a sacred custom, he deliberately struck up a conversation with this woman.

Jesus was not prejudiced against this Samaritan because she was a woman. Sexism had no place in his evangelism. In fact, Jesus was the true liberator of women. He was the only one who truly set women free. Nobody has ever done for women what Jesus did and does for them.

A second strike which the Samaritan woman had against her was her religion. She worshiped God through a false religion. All of the talk in John 4 about where people ought to worship is not extraneous. It is very much to the point. The Samaritans had built a temple on Mount Gerizim to rival the one on Mount Zion in Jerusalem. They had set up their own priesthood and had their own Bible. The Samaritan Pentateuch is different from the Jewish Pentateuch. Clearly this woman was seeking to worship God through a false religion.

Please notice that Jesus did not refuse to talk with the woman because of her false religion. Yet, how often when we meet one who tells us he or she is a Buddhist or a Hindu, we clam up and refuse to talk with such persons. Or, more likely a person rings our door bell and says: ''I am a Jehovah's Witness,'' or ''I am a member of the Church of Jesus Christ of the Latter Day Saints.'' How do we respond to such groups? Do we slam the door? Do we manage to say, ''I see,'' or ''Oh'' or ''I'm not interested''?

Jesus showed a profound respect for this woman in spite of her false religion. He readily entered into a dialogue with her. If we are to pattern our witnessing after Jesus, we shall exhibit the same kind of respect and willingly enter into similar kinds of conversation with today's adherents of false religions and heretical sects.

A third strike which she had against her was her sexual immorality. She had had five husbands, and the man with whom she was then living was not her husband. That sounds more like today than Palestine in the first century. There is no doubt about it. This woman was the town prostitute. That's the reason she came to draw water at noon instead of in the late afternoon. She did not come when the other women came because they would have ostracized her. She may have even stolen some of their husbands from them.

But please notice that Jesus did not refuse to talk with the woman because she was a prostitute. He didn't start running out across the desert when he saw her coming. He didn't cry out? "Don't come near me; don't contaminate me with your sinfulness." How on earth shall we ever convert real sinners to Jesus Christ if we refuse to come into contact with them?

Several years ago I read about a seminary student who witnessed in bars every Friday night for his field work assignment. One night he had taken a position at a table alone and was drinking a soft drink and reading his New Testament. A buxom young brunette from the Orient, who was advertised as "Zaka the Great," the belly dancer in the establishment, slinked over to him to chat. When she saw his Bible, she exclaimed, "What are you doing here?"

He said that he was studying to be a minister and that he cared for people who had problems. He asked her if she knew of anyone with a problem he might possibly help.

"Well," she said haltingly, "I do have a friend with a problem." She explained that her "friend" had a boyfriend, and the two of them were living together in the "friend's" apartment. The problem was that the young man would neither marry the "friend," nor could she get him to move out. Then the dancer made an embarrassing slip: "I just wish that he would give her back the key to my apartment, uh, I mean her apartment." She began to cry. Then she described the unhappiness of her life and how she had been exploited in plying her trade. Deep within her heart she had wanted to be loved, really loved by someone.

When the seminarian told her about Christ's love for her, her face revealed the depth of the loneliness of her heart. After a long pause, she abruptly left him, but not without taking with her his New Testament.

Some people might think a Christian should not frequent bars.

We might even be afraid of what others might say about us if we are seen in such places. I think it is possible that we can get to feeling so holy about our own goodness and so concerned over our own reputations that we become too "holy" for God to use. Most sinners will not come to us; we have to go to them. They refuse to meet us on our turf and on our terms. Could it be possible that Jesus wants us to seek them out on their turf as did the seminary student?

A fourth strike which the Samaritan woman had against her was her race. The fact that she was a Samaritan meant that she was half-Jew and the other half God alone knew. The Samaritans had frequently intermarried with their foreign conquerors. They were, what we would call in the vernacular, half-breeds, or mongrel Jews.

The racial prejudice of Jews toward Samaritans, and vice versa, was very intense. In fact, Jews had no social dealings with Samaritans. Jews who had to travel from Judea to Galilee would usually not take the shortest route through Samaria, a fact which we might think especially important because most travel was then on foot or beast. Rather, they took the long route, crossed over the Jordan at Jericho and went up the east bank of Jordan and thus bypassed Samaria.

The intense hatred of Jews for Samaritans may be seen in what the enemies of Jesus said about him in John 8:48. When Jesus' enemies wanted to say the worst thing they could about him, they said: "Are we not right in saying that you are a Samaritan and have a demon?" In other words: You are a half-breed; you are not a true Jew; you are possessed by a demon.

But please notice that Jesus was not hung up on racism. He went through Samaria. He asked the woman for a drink of water. Wherever Jesus dealt with Samaritans or spoke to them, he did so with kindness and respect. For example, in Luke 9:51-56, two of Jesus' disciples wanted to call down fire from heaven and wipe a Samaritan village off the map because that village refused to welcome Jesus. Jesus rebuked them. Also, the most beautiful story Jesus ever told made a Samaritan its hero (see Luke 10:29-37). Furthermore, of the ten lepers whom Jesus healed, the only one who turned back and thanked him was a Samaritan (see Luke 17:11-19).

By way of summary, the woman at the well had her sex against her, her religion against her, her morals against her, and her race against her. All of these things were against her, but Jesus was for her.

Implications

If we would pattern our evangelism after that of Jesus, we will show the same respect for personality which he did. The very first issue which we must settle is our attitude toward persons. If we don't believe persons are worth saving, we will not so much as lift one little finger to save them.

If we truly respect personality, we shall ascribe infinite worth to every human being. When God creates a person, he writes on him or her a price tag which reads: Of Infinite Worth, Not for Sale!

If we truly respect personality, we shall refuse to run over, manipulate, or coerce people. The decision which we seek is an autonomous one. People who use offensive methods of witnessing are playing the averages rather than being concerned about individual persons.

If we truly respect personality, we shall refuse to argue or pressure people into the church. Ralph Sockman was right, "An ounce of honest testimony is worth a ton of argument." Persons enter the kingdom of God through faith in Jesus Christ, not because they have been overpowered by clever arguments. If people are to be pressured at all, let it be the pressure of the Holy Spirit.

The above two implications are so important that I should like to belabor them just a bit. God does not expect us to be steamrollers or juggernauts.

One man, about whom I heard, went to see a prospect in the morning. His potential disciple was a man who happened to be working on the third shift that week. The prospect's wife told the visitor that her husband was sleeping because he had worked the "graveyard" shift the previous night. Instead of the witness excusing himself and seeking to come back at a more convenient time, he insisted that the wife show him to the bed where his prospect was sleeping. Having awakened the gentleman, he then proceeded to witness to him.

Unless God strongly leads us to do something like that, I caution against it. Some of us are not aggressive enough; nevertheless, it is possible for us to be too pushy and thus invade a person's privacy.

An incident happened in the first Lay Evangelism School which I attended that has made me more sensitive to respect for personality. Three of our witnesses called at a home one evening where the prospect was taking a bath. The man on the team asked the prospect's wife where the bathroom was. He barged into the bathroom and proceeded to try to witness to the man who was actually taking a bath. The prospect kept trying to say: "I'd rather you would come back and talk with me at a more convenient time." Finally, the visitor got the message, left the little green booklet on the back of the commode, and came on back to the church to tell us what had happened.

The thing which shocked me so much about that experience was that so many people at the church thought the visitor had done the right thing! The majority of them literally applauded him and commended him on his courage. I thought to myself, *How insensitive can we get! Will anyone ever be able to win that man now that his privacy has been invaded?*

Dr. Jack Stanton gave me the sequel to this true story. That prospect was later introduced to Christ and joined the church. So God can and does overrule our mistakes. However, I caution against such offensive methods which may violate one's personality.

If we truly respect personality, we shall listen to people. John Drakeford spoke truly when he wrote about *The Awesome Power of the Listening Ear.*[3] James 1:19 says, "Let every man be swift to hear, slow to speak." A limerick which we sometime quote is very apropos to our witnessing: "Two eyes, two ears have we each, but only one mouth designed for speech; therefore, let us look and listen twice as much before attempting to vocalize." I once heard a person say: "Evangelism is listening to someone until he tells you his U. C. [Ultimate Concern], then you tell him about your J. C. [Jesus Christ]." Such a definition may not be too far afield.

Dietrich Bonhoeffer told us in *Life Together* that the first service we Christians owe another person is to listen to him or her. Even business corporations are beginning to understand and to capitalize upon the importance of listening. Sperry Univac launched an advertising and public relations campaign in 1979 which says, "We understand how important it is to listen."[4]

Listening is extremely difficult, if not impossible, for persons who have a stomach full of problems. Persons who need to "dump their bucket," to get things off their chest, or are in pain have to have a catharsis before they can be persuaded to do anything. A skillful listener may help such persons.

If we truly respect personality, we shall be kind to people. Ian McLaren once said, "Be kind to every person you meet; he is having a hard time." Henry Thoreau may have at least been in the ball park when he suggested that most people live lives of quiet desperation. I do not take McLaren or Thoreau nearly so seriously as I do the apostle Paul who commanded us to "be kind to one another" (Eph. 4:32). If there is anyone on earth who ought to be kind to others, it is the one who has experienced the kindness of God in Jesus Christ.

If we truly respect personality, we shall not become impatient with those who express to us their honest doubts. I know there is such a thing as dishonest doubt. But honest doubt can be on the cutting edge of faith. Tennyson said, "There is more faith in honest doubt than in your creeds." Jesus did not become impatient with Nicodemus' doubt when he inquired, "How can these things be?"

One reason I believe the Bible is inspired by God is that it doesn't gloss over the weaknesses of even the twelve. In the closing scene of Matthew's Gospel, Jesus came to the eleven in Galilee. Matthew says, "but some doubted" (28:17). I think many people in our time are right where the father of the epileptic boy was when he said, "I believe; help my unbelief" (Mark 9:24). Isn't there a verse somewhere which says of the Messiah, "a bruised reed he will not break, and a dimly burning wick he will not quench"?

One further implication of the dignity principle is that if we truly respect personality numbers may be put in a different light. Soʹren Kierkegaard seemed certain that "Christianity is in inverse proportion to numbers." On the contrary, consider what Charles Livingstone says:

The difference between 97 and 98 persons reached this year is one invaluable soul! The difference between 15 and 16 persons reached may be one divided home, one child whose father needs Christ and Christian fellowship, or one youth whose potential for spiritual leadership goes undeveloped.[5]

If numbers are shorthand for persons, then it behooves us to be concerned about numbers.

Conclusion

We ought to ask of every method we use: Does this method respect personality? If it doesn't, that method is suspect and ought either to be abandoned or changed so that it does respect personality. We are too accustomed to asking the question: Will it work? Prior to the pragmatic test is the ethical and theological test. Before we ask: Will it work, we ought to ask: Is it right? Does it respect personality? Long-term gains ought to concern us as much or more than short-term gains.

Notes

1. Leighton Ford, *The Christian Persuader* (New York: Harper & Row, Publishers, 1966), p. 67.

2. Quoted by Frank and Evelyn Stagg, *Woman in the World of Jesus* (Philadelphia: The Westminster Press, 1978), p. 10. See also Melanie Morrison, "Jesus and Women," *Sojourners,* Vol. 9, No. 7, July, 1980, pp. 11-14.

3. See John Drakeford, *The Awesome Power of the Listening Ear* (Waco, Texas: Word Books, 1967).

4. See Beth Ann Krier, "When Listening, Few People Are All Ears," *The Kansas City Times,* Feb. 12, 1981, pp. A-1 and A-12.

5. Charles Livingstone, *Using the Sunday School to Reach People* (Nashville: Convention Press, 1973), p. 9.

3
Enfleshment

Theme: Jesus fleshed out the gospel in his own body and life-style
Scripture Lesson: Isaiah 7:14; John 1:14-18

Introduction

A second principle of evangelism according to Christ is what I call the enfleshment principle. This is the principle of fleshing out the gospel with our own flesh and blood and bones—the principle of incarnating in our lives the message which we verbalize with our lips.

The gospel does need a voice. However, it needs a body also. The Word has to become flesh in us.

Jesus not only spoke the gospel and did the gospel but also he was the gospel. As John said, "The Word became flesh and dwelt among us" (John 1:14). If we would pattern our evangelism after Jesus Christ, somehow the good news about the kingdom of God must become flesh in us. Not, of course, in the same unique sense as it became flesh in Jesus of Nazareth. He was the "only begotten Son of God," the only one of his kind. Nevertheless, the gospel must permeate the marrow of our bones, flow through the blood of our veins, and become wrapped up with our skin so that we become living extensions of the incarnation.

Verbal proclamation of the gospel is a supplement to the incarnation of it. Words, even true and holy words, must never become a substitute to the enfleshing of the good news.

Fingers Pointing to Enfleshment

Martin Luther was not being irreverent when he said every Christian ought to be a Christ to his neighbor. Jesus himself said, "As the

Father has sent me, even so I send you'' (John 20:21). Every Christian ought to be a living sample of the gospel. We can't witness adequately to the incarnation of Jesus Christ until the Word of God has been incarnated in us. A disembodied word is not sufficient for our world.

The late Marshall McLuhan made famous the phrase, ''The medium is the message.'' That was certainly true of Jesus, and it is true of us. Jesus was God's message enfleshed. We Christians are also living demonstrations of God's intention for humanity. Next to Jesus of Nazareth, we are the best examples which God has in the world.

The 1980 Consultation on World Evangelization, held in Pattaya, Thailand, issued what was called ''The Thailand Statement.'' One section of that statement calls for integrity in the character and conduct of the gospel-bearer. It reads:

Our witness loses credibility when we contradict it by our life or life-style. Our light will shine only when others can see our good works (Matt. 5:16). In a word, if we are to speak of Jesus with integrity, we have to resemble him.[1]

I think Paul may have had something like this in mind when he posited the doctrine of Christ as the Second Adam. We Christians are not Adam I people; we are Adam II people. The formation of Christ in us is a new kind of incarnation.

We may not realize it, but every Christian is a living letter, ''known and read by all men'' (2 Cor. 3:2). We are, like it or not, personal demonstrations of the gospel.

E. M. Bounds has said, ''Men are God's method.''[2] If that is true, perhaps what we need is not so much better methods as better people.

Robert Coleman points out that evangelism is not done by *something,* but by *someone.* Words, even biblical words, are insufficient in themselves. Our words have to take on flesh and blood. Coleman continues:

The Gospel concerns Someone, not something. It can never become an abstract theory or mechanical program since it is an expression of God's love, and God is a Person. Some methodology must be used in getting the message across, but the hand that extends the invitation is flesh and blood.[3]

There can be no substitute for enfleshing the gospel. Ernie ("Tex") Prichard relates a humorous story which makes this point. A young man was determined to get his girl friend to marry him. Being a rather bashful fellow, every day he sent her a letter of proposal. Each day without fail that love note was mailed. Finally, after three weeks of that, his girl friend did get married; but she married the postman![4]

J. I. Packer is in the same thought vein when he writes that "the key to persuasive Christian communication lies less in technique than in character."[5] Those who enflesh the gospel will witness from a base of strength. Our world is satiated with all kind of messages. In our kind of context, that message which takes on flesh and blood will be heard more readily than a disembodied word.

Henry Drummond goes so far as to suggest that man himself was originally a word made flesh![6] "God's truth will not go into a word," said Drummond. "You must put it in an image. God Himself could not put truth in a word, therefore He made the Word flesh."[7]

This principle of enfleshment may be seen to some extent in a Roman Catholic television magazine show which debuted in the fall of 1980. Producer Martin Doblmeir says the thrust of the show is "evangelization through example." The pilot program focused upon Washington, D.C., priest Horace McKenna's work among the city's poor.[8]

Hallam, the subject of Tennyson's "In Memoriam," said, "I like Christianity because it fits into all the folds of one's nature." That's what is meant by enfleshing the gospel—fitting it into all the folds of one's nature. In fact when all is said and done in evangelism, we need to remember that "the attestation of Christianity is the Christian."[9]

Perhaps one of the best ways to understand this principle of enfleshment is to examine it in the light of the incarnation of Christ. Very clearly, fleshing out the good news has something to do with the Christian doctrine of the incarnation.

Most of us probably know more about the crucifixion, the resurrection, and the second coming of Christ than we know about his incarnation. We may even know more about the ascension than the incarnation. These other aspects of Christology have more content for us than does the incarnation.

Our theologians, up until the last few decades, have said more about the crucifixion, resurrection, ascension, and second coming than they have about the incarnation. That was not true, however, of the first several centuries of the church's history. The early church debated how the two natures of God and man could be perfectly conjoined in the one person, Jesus of Nazareth. But since then until about the rise of Nazism, the doctrine of the incarnation has not been a lively issue with most of us.

Therefore, I freely confess that I don't know a great deal about the incarnation. It remains a mystery to me. Nevertheless, I do know four things about the incarnation.

Identification

God identified himself with persons in the incarnation. That's the first thing I know about it. The prophecy which said his name should be called Immanuel (Isa. 7:14), or "God with us," was fulfilled in the incarnation.

God did not just become a man in general in the incarnation. He became the man Jesus of Nazareth. He became a particular man in a particular time and place. He became a Jew in first-century Palestine. Hence, God did not become a Samaritan, nor a Greek, nor a Scot, nor an American.[10]

God limited himself in the incarnation. He limited himself to human nature and to a specific culture. He limited himself to the servant role and to the cross death. To be sure, God's limitation was self-imposed. As Paul put it, he "emptied himself" (Phil. 2:7).

Nevertheless, the limits were real. The universal took on particularity. The abstract became concrete. The invisible became visible. God's face was unveiled and made known. "The Word became flesh" (John 1:14). God took on human form.

That is probably what Reinhold Niebuhr meant when he told us that the incarnation constitutes "the scandal of particularity." Incarnation was, indeed, a scandal to the Gnostics. Some of them even went so far as to deny that Jesus left footprints as he walked on the wet sand of a seashore! They said he only *seemed* to be a man. Believing that matter was intrinsically evil, the Gnostics could not accept the full humanity of the Christ.

Evangelicals believe so strongly in the deity of Christ that they have not fully grasped the radical nature of God's identification with humanity in the incarnation. We tend toward Gnosticism in our Christology. That tendency toward heresy is precisely why we need to remind ourselves that it is just as heretical to deny the full humanity of Jesus as it is to deny his full deity. "When He made the Word flesh, when He made Jesus a Man, He made a *Man*," wrote Henry Drummond.[11]

We dare not minimize the humanity of our Lord. Does not the incarnation of Jesus suggest a comparable, particular identification in our evangelism? It is insufficient for us merely to enflesh the gospel in some vague, general fashion. We need to flesh it out in our time and place. Otherwise, we cannot identify with those whom we seek to convert.

There is an old Indian proverb which says, "One man should say nothing to another until he has walked in his moccasins." God walked in our moccasins in the incarnation.

Like Ezekiel, God sat where we sit in the incarnation. And that's the reason the writer of Hebrews could say: "For we have not a high priest who is unable to sympathize with our weaknesses, but one who in every respect has been tempted as we are, yet without sin. Let us then with confidence draw near to the throne of grace, that we may receive mercy and find grace to help in time of need" (4:15-16). We don't face anything which God has not already faced in the incarnation of his Son.

If we pattern our evangelism after Jesus Christ, we too shall seek to thoroughly identify ourselves with those whom we would convert. We ought to so thoroughly identify ourselves with their plight that they will know we do understand their situation and that we care greatly for them and for their welfare.

When John Wesley went to Savannah, Georgia, there were 518 souls in that place. They were an assortment of the wealthy, Indians, slaves, and poor folk. That first Sunday as Wesley preached, he observed that some of his congregation wore no shoes. The next Sunday and every Sunday thereafter Wesley reportedly appeared barefooted in his pulpit so long as he was in Georgia.[12] That is one example of the lengths to which one might go in order to identify with those whom he loves.

John R. W. Stott recognized the need for identification with our prospects when he said, "All true evangelism demands a kind of incarnation, an entering into other people's worlds, into their pain and suffering, into their loneliness and lostness, and even into their thought world."[13]

Father Damien showed us what enfleshment means when he so perfectly identified himself with the lepers which he served that one day he himself became a leper. On that day the priest was able to address the leper colony by saying: "We lepers. . . ." Father Damien's ministry among the lepers incarnated the love of Christ.

Visibility

A second fact which I understand about the incarnation is that in it God became visible. God got where people could see him, touch him, feel him. Prior to the incarnation, no one had ever seen God, but now in it, "the only Son, who is in the bosom of the Father, he has made him known" (John 1:18). He has exegeted him; he has unveiled him.

The writer of Hebrews put it, "He reflects the glory of God and bears the very stamp of his nature" (1:3). When persons saw Jesus of Nazareth, they were looking at one who showed them God.

Rachel Richardson Smith has used pregnancy to explain this mystery of the incarnation. A pregnant woman is intricately bound up with her baby, though she is distinct from it. Herein lies the paradox. The two are one; the pregnant woman is both herself and the baby. Yet, as Smith says, "The two are distinct from each other, though they are not separate." Smith continues:

This too is the paradox of incarnation. God and Christ are the two in one. God is both Christ and other than Christ. Though not separate from Christ, God is distinct from Christ. Christ does not contain God. Christ is not all of God, as the newborn baby is not all of the mother. But in Christ, God gives birth to God.[14]

"God solved the problem of his own invisibility," said John R. W. Stott, "in the coming of Jesus Christ, who was the visible image of the invisible God."[15] God solves the problem of his invisibility today by making himself visible in individual Christians and in the visible Christian community. Every Christian and every church ought to be a visible demonstration of the power of the gospel.

If we imitate this principle of enfleshment in our evangelism, we too shall make God visible to persons. We shall become living demonstrations of God's intention for humanity. This may have been a part of what Paul meant when he called some of his converts living epistles known and read by all (see 2 Cor. 3:1-3). Some people may never read the gospel according to Matthew, Mark, Luke, and John. But as an unknown poet has well said:

> You are writing each day a letter
>   to men;
> Take care that the writing is
>   true;
> 'Tis the only gospel that some
>   men will read . . .
> That gospel according to you.

We are told that the eyes retain an average of 87 percent of what they see; the ears 11 percent of what they hear; and the other senses 2 percent. Moreover, the eye is said to be 22 times faster than the ear in transmitting images to the brain.

If those figures are anywhere close to being accurate, they throw the words of an eloquent, but unknown, black preacher into a very favorable light: "Our walk ought to match our talk. We ought to walk our talk; and we ought to talk our walk. For our walk talks, and our talk walks."

Russell Begaye, a missionary who was born and reared on a

Navajo reservation in New Mexico, puts the visibility of the incarnation in a unique way. Begaye suggests we should have the ears of Jesus, the eyes of Jesus, the feet of Jesus, the hands of Jesus, and so forth. If we are a continuation of his incarnation, we shall seek to be his body in the world.

Where is God today? Mother Teresa in 1948 ventured out of the cloister into some of the most infamous and horrible slums of the world. She exclaimed:

Such a beautiful day: to meet Christ face to face in the poor. He was there, the hungry Christ, the naked Christ, the sick Christ, the homeless Christ—the touch of him in this distressing disguise gave me great joy and peace and strength.[16]

I am not so sure about seeing God in such distressing disguises as is Mother Teresa. However, I know that one place where persons ought to be able to see God is in you and me who name the name of Christ and who wear the label *Christian*.

The name given to the Christ child was Immanuel, which means "God is with us." Precisely because we Christians are extensions of the incarnation, we too are given the name "God is with us." Whatever else may be your name, if you are a Christian, your name is also Immanuel. Insofar as the church is an extension of the incarnation, it too goes by the name Immanuel. If our lives do not fit our name, we should change our lives so that they do match our lofty name.

I like much better what Mother Teresa says about the other side of incarnating the love of God, "Today in this world God has made us to be his love and compassion."[17] There are persons who have forgotten the gentle human touch. There are even those who have forgotten how to smile. We Christians are called to be God's love and compassion to all such "little" brothers and sisters.

Vulnerability

A third fact which I understand about the incarnation is that in it God became vulnerable. God in the incarnation got where people could place a crown of thorns on his head, beat him with their hands, drive nails into his hands and feet, thrust a spear into his side, and kill him. He abandoned his safety and security and fully exposed himself to people.

Let me ask you something. What is more vulnerable than a little baby, completely dependent upon someone else to care for him? Yet, that is the way God chose to come into the world, as the babe of Bethlehem. Both the cradle and the cross witness to God's vulnerability.

I am suggesting that if we imitate Jesus Christ in our evangelism, we too will become vulnerable to people. We shall have to abandon our false safety and security and expose our true selves to people. The world has a right to know where we stand on all of the burning issues of our day. One reason the world is rotting is that Christians are refusing to be salt. But when we expose our true selves and our deepest thoughts and feelings, we run the risk of getting hurt or of being rejected. So what, is the servant greater than his master?

Betty King's ''Poem for Good Friday and After'' catches this point:

> There you hung
> Way out on a sawed-off limb
> Inviting us to go out on a limb
>   and saw it off and take it up
> And follow You.
> Here we come.[18]

The principle of enfleshment implies a readiness to lay our very bodies on the line for Christ. It may even lead to death and martyrdom. The story about the forty martyrs of Sebaste, while it belongs to the fourth century AD, might well be rewritten with our own blood in this twentieth century.

These forty soldiers were all Christians. They were members of the famous Twelfth Legion of Rome's imperial army. Suddenly, they were told by their captain that their Emperor Licinius had issued an edict which required all soldiers to offer sacrifice to the pagan gods. These forty Christian soldiers replied: ''You can have our armor and even our bodies, but our heart's allegiance belongs to Jesus Christ.''

The time of year was mid-winter, AD 320. The captain had them marched out to a nearby frozen lake. They were stripped of their clothes and told to either renounce Christ or die. During the night the men huddled together singing their song, "Forty Martyrs for Christ." Slowly, the temperature took its toll. One by one they fell to the ice.

Finally, only one man was left. His courage failed him, and he stumbled to shore renouncing Christ. However, the officer over the guards had been watching all this. Unknown to the others, he had secretly come to believe in Christ. When the officer saw the last man break rank, he walked out into the frozen lake, removed his clothes, and confessed that he also was a Christian.

As the sun rose the next morning, there were forty bodies on the ice.[19] The blood of the martyrs is still the seed of the church. It is not without significance that our word for *witness* comes from a Greek root from which we also get our word *martyr.*

I am suggesting that there is an element of risk in evangelism. God risked himself in the incarnation. If we are in dead earnest in our evangelism, we shall also risk ourselves.

Contextualization

A fourth point which I am beginning to understand about the incarnation is that in it God contextualized our salvation. Theologians are now calling this contextualization. God, in other words, offers us salvation in our particular cultural setting. We don't have to conform to some other person's cultural image in order to be saved. The only image to which we need to conform is the image of God's beloved Son.[20]

The principle of enfleshment necessarily involves contextualization, vulnerability, visibility, and identification. Evangelization is a costly enterprise.

Conclusion

Evangelism should be seen in the light of divine exemplarism. God gave us a perfect evangelist in Jesus of Nazareth. Jesus exemplifies the type of evangelist God wants.

The first sentence of the Book of Acts reads: "In the first book, O

Theophilus, I have dealt with all that Jesus began to do and teach"
(1:1). Usually we put that the other way around and say, "Practice
what you teach." Here the beloved physician, Luke, said that Jesus
taught what he practiced! Indeed, the divine order seems to be "Do
and Tell" rather than "Tell and Do." We teach best by example and
conduct. Our modeling is more powerful than our methods.

It is said of the parson in Chaucer's Canterbury Tales, "This good
example to his sheep he brought that first he wrought, and afterwards
he taught." Surely, there is biblical sanction for that pattern in Acts
1:1.

B. B. McKinney sort of sums up what I have been trying to say
about enfleshing the gospel in the first two stanzas of his hymn: "Let
Others See Jesus in You."[21]

> While passing thro' this world of sin,
> And others your life shall view,
> Be clean and pure without, within,
> Let others see Jesus in you.
>
> Your life's a book before their eyes,
> They're reading it thro' and thro';
> Say, does it point them to the skies,
> Do others see Jesus in you?

Notes

1. *World Evangelization,* Information Bulletin No. 20, Sept., 1980, p. 7. This is a
publication of the Lausanne Committee for World Evangelization. "The Thailand
Statement" will be found in full on pp. 6-7.

2. Quoted by Robert E. Coleman, *The Master Plan of Evangelism* (Westwood, New
Jersey: Fleming H. Revell Co., 1963), p. 113.

3. Robert E. Coleman, *They Meet the Master* (Huntington Valley, Penn.: Christian
Outreach, 1973), p. 8.

4. Ernie Prichard, *Salesmanship for Christ* (Nashville: Broadman Press, 1972), p.
31.

5. James I. Packer, "The Gospel—Its Content and Communication: A Theological

Perspective," in John Stott and Robert T. Coote, eds., *Gospel & Culture* (Pasadena, Calif.: Wm. Carey Library, 1979), p. 151.

6. Henry Drummond, *The New Evangelism* (London: Hodder and Stoughton, 1899), pp. 30-31.

7. Ibid., p. 29.

8. Reported in *Christianity Today*, XXIV, No. 15 (Sept. 5, 1980), p. 85.

9. Drummond, p. 108.

10. See I. Howard Marshall's "Culture and the New Testament," in John Stott and Robert T. Coote, eds., *Gospel & Culture* (Pasadena, Calif.: 1979), p. 30.

11. Drummond, p. 17.

12. Related by Elbert Hubbard, *Little Journeys to the Homes of Great Reformers,* Vol. XX (East Aurora, New York: The Roycrofters, 1907), pp. 19-20.

13. Quoted in *World Evangelization,* Information Bulletin No. 18, p. 1, a publication of the Lausanne Committee for World Evangelization.

14. Quoted by W. Randall Lolley in *Outlook,* January-February, 1981, p. 2, the Southeastern Baptist Theological Seminary Bulletin.

15. Quoted in *World Evangelization,* Information Bulletin No. 18, p. 2, a publication of the Lausanne Committee for World Evangelization.

16. Quoted by Jack A. Jennings, "A Reluctant Demurrer on Mother Teresa," *The Christian Century,* XCVIII, No. 8, Mar. 11, 1981, p. 258.

17. Mother Teresa, "God's Understanding Love," *Seeds,* Vol. 4, No. 2, 1981, p. 8.

18. Betty King, "Poem for Good Friday and After," p. 421. Copyright 1981 Christian Century Foundation. Reprinted by permission from the April 15, 1981 issue of *The Christian Century.*

19. Related by Leighton Ford, "What Are You Afraid Of?" *Decision,* Dec., 1978 (Vol. 19, No. 12), p. 4.

20. I am indebted to C. Norman Kraus for suggesting this idea. See C. Norman Kraus, "Today's Gospel of Salvation," in C. Norman Kraus, ed., *Missions, Evangelism, and Church Growth* (Scottdale, Penn.: Herald Press, 1980), p. 79.

21. B. B. McKinney, "Let Others See Jesus in You," *Baptist Hymnal,* 1975, No. 294. Copyright 1924. Renewal 1952 Broadman Press. All rights reserved.

4

Uniqueness

Theme: Jesus dealt with each person as a unique creation of God
Scripture Lesson: Psalm 8:3-9; Matthew 19:16-22

Introduction

A third principle of evangelism according to Christ is that of uniqueness. Jesus dealt with every person as a unique individual. He never dealt with any two persons exactly alike. He did not have one speech which he went around parroting to every person whom he met, as though he were a robot or a stuck record.

Examples from the Evangelism of Jesus

Jesus suited his message to the needs of his hearers. He said to Nicodemus, the high-born intellectual of Israel: "You must be born anew" (John 3:7). But there is no record he ever said that to anyone else. That was what Nicodemus needed to hear.

Jesus "knew what was in man" (John 2:25). He read Nicodemus like a book. He knew Nicodemus was extremely self-conscious about his birth and heritage. So he addressed himself to the unique needs of this "blue blood" of Israel. See how he correlated his message to the uniqueness of his hearers.

Jesus said to the rich young ruler, "If you would be perfect, go, sell what you possess and give to the poor, and you will have treasure in heaven; and come, follow me" (Matt. 19:21). But there is no record he said that to anyone else. That was what the rich young ruler needed to hear.

This was one who had "great possessions" and knew not the true riches. Jesus read him accurately and addressed him accordingly.

Nevertheless, this man who had everything but the one thing needful, "went away sorrowful." Again, see how Jesus correlated his message to the uniqueness of his potential disciples.

Take another example from the evangelism of Jesus. A woman who had been caught in the very act of adultery was cast in his presence. Her accusers demanded, "What do you say about her?" Jesus wrote something with his finger on the ground. To her accusers he said, "Let him who is without sin among you be the first to throw a stone at her" (John 8:7). To the frightened woman, he said, "Neither do I condemn you; go, and do not sin again" (John 8:11).

There is certainly no record that Jesus said that to anyone else. As a matter of fact, some manuscripts do not even include the incident! The Revised Standard Version relegates it to a footnote.

See how Jesus suited his message to the unique needs and circumstances of his hearers. A high-born intellectual is told he must be born again. A young man who had everything is told to sell all. An adulteress is told that she is not condemned but to go and stop sinning.

These examples are chosen almost at random. They are not exceptions. They are the rule. To a man blind from birth, our Lord said, "Go, wash in the pool of Siloam" (John 9:7). To a sick man at the pool of Bethzatha, Jesus said, "Do you want to be healed?" (John 5:6). To an official whose son was at the point of death, Jesus said, "Go; your son will live" (John 4:50).

Surely, we can see how Jesus began with persons where they were. He began with them where they were socially, morally, religiously, educationally, physically, and so forth. While he sought to lead them into the kingdom, he did so by relating what he said and did to their unique personalities and to their particular needs and peculiar circumstances.

Application of the Principle

If we apply the principle of uniqueness in our witnessing, we too will begin with persons where they are. We shall respect their uniqueness and suit our message to their particular needs.

For example, we shall not deal with the tenderhearted, twelve-year-old girl in the same way we deal with the hardened fifty-year-old male criminal. Jesus himself told of one who was just outside the door of the kingdom of God and of another who was a prodigal living in a far country. Some persons are just outside the kingdom, while others are a thousand miles from it. Some are warm and receptive; others are cold and indifferent. Some are under the conviction of the Holy Spirit; others are souls on ice. Common sense, as well as the way Jesus dealt with persons, teaches us to deal with each person as a unique creation of God.

We don't go out to an orchard and pick green fruit; we pick ripe fruit. Much in the same manner, we shouldn't pluck the green prospects. We cultivate them, get to know them, meet their needs, and become their friends. Then, when the harvest time comes, we pluck the ripe fruit for God. Only by beginning with persons where they are in their pilgrimages can we bear fruit that abides (see John 15:16).

"God is a God of variety," said Henry Drummond. "No two leaves are the same, no two sand grains, no two souls."[1] We might add that no two snowflakes are the same, no two sets of finger prints, and no two sets of voice prints. Aren't you thankful that God is not in the cloning business? The God who has made nature and human nature with such variety expects us to celebrate that gift and to take notice of such uniqueness in our evangelism.

No two persons are exactly alike—not even identical twins. So, we can't deal with any two persons exactly alike in our evangelism. "The God who allows no two snowflakes to share a common design," writes Ken Anderson, "wants to give freshness and spontaneity to each experience."[2]

Nobody can teach us one set speech or one cut and dried formula which can be used in every witnessing encounter. If so, witness might become rigmarole.

I have been told that when the Jehovah's Witnesses began, they would go from door to door with a hand-cranked Gramophone and ask each person to listen to the recording which they played. They still go from house to house, but now they evidently memorize their speeches. That is quite an improvement. Nevertheless, if you interrupt a new Jehovah's Witness in the early part of his speech, he might have to go back and repeat some of what he had said in order to locate his place.

This is related not to put down the zealous members of a sect. I would to God that we had more of that kind of zeal. If we had their zeal, we would lead more persons to the Savior. My point is to say that God does not expect us to become automatons or robots in our evangelism. He doesn't expect us to play the same speech to every potential convert as though we were some stuck or damaged record. The witness is not some giant parrot who goes around repeating, "Polly wants a cracker." That would be an insult to others, to ourselves, and to our Creator who has lavished such variety upon his creation.

Rebecca Pippert has written a remarkable book which assures us that "we can choose a style comfortable for us" in our witnessing.[3] We don't have to become somebody else or violate anyone else's God-given uniqueness in order to be effective witnesses.

Pippert's book is really about a "second turning." In our "first turning," we are transformed from caterpillars into butterflies, from natural people into spiritual people. That is the turning of the new birth. However, in order to become effective witnesses, we need to have "a second turning in which the spiritual person again becomes natural." Pippert does not want us to turn the evangelism department of the church into the sales department. She wants us to depend more upon communication through personality than through techniques and strategy.[4]

While I see an important role for techniques and strategy in evangelism, I am quick to affirm that evangelism is most effective when it is seen as a way of life. To say the very least, the principle of uniqueness should teach us that just as there are varieties of fish, so a variety of fishing methods might be in order. As a matter of fact, no one fishing method will appeal to every fisherman; nor will any one method catch all of the fish. Hence, not only is every fish unique; every person who fishes is also unique.

The one thing for certain is that "we must begin with people where they are, rather than where we would like for them to be.'' That is the considered opinion of Great Britain's Donald Lord Soper, one of the most experienced witnesses to secular unchurched persons in our lifetime.[5] Moreover, this appears to have been a great undergirding principle which guided Jesus in his evangelizing.

Paul seemed to recognize this principle of uniqueness. He counseled the Colossians to behave toward unbelievers "so that you may know how you ought to answer every one" (Col. 4:6). Not every person is asking the same question. Our answers should correspond to a person's questions. We should in our evangelism, to use the vernacular, scratch where persons are itching.

Paul's teaching on the principle of uniqueness is in the category of "Do as I do," not just "Do as I say." He said in 1 Corinthians 9:19-23 that he accommodated himself to the uniqueness of his prospects: "To the Jews I became as a Jew," "to those under the law I became as one under the law," "to those outside the law I became as one outside the law," and "to the weak I became weak."

Paul's evangelism in Athens (see Acts 17:22-34) reveals how much he respected the uniqueness of his hearers. He did not blame or offend his audience. He did not begin in a manner that would excite prejudice or opposition. He introduced the worship of an unknown god not as a matter of blame but as proof of their devotion to religion. The entire speech is "calm, dignified, and argumentative—such as became such a place, such a speaker, and such an audience."[6]

Had Jesus not followed the principle of uniqueness in his evangelism, he would have had considerable difficulty in communicating with his receptors. The principle of uniqueness recognizes the cultural and language differences in human beings.

Jesus spoke to the woman at the well about water which would quench her thirst forever. He talked to the fishermen, whom he called, in terms of fishing for people. He spoke to the rich young ruler in monetary terms. He met persons where they were and seemed to suit his language to their context.

Some Christians once thought that the New Testament was written in a special "Holy Ghost" language. They found that it was not like the classical Greek of Homer and Socrates. They could find nothing with which to compare New Testament Greek. Then, papyri were discovered which had been written in the same kind of Greek as the New Testament. Business documents and love letters were found which used *Koine* Greek. Christians were amazed to find that their New Testament was the common Greek of the common people.

The principle of uniqueness requires that we use a language which persons can understand. A minister of youth tells how a young girl returned from Heavenly Haven Camp and ran to the kitchen to tell her mother the good news. "Hey, Mom, I've been saved!"

"But Betty Jean," her mother replied, "you're a great swimmer, why did you almost drown?"

"No, Mom, you don't understand. My counselor gave an 'invitation.' "

"An invitation to what?"

"An invitation to 'walk the aisle' and be 'born again.' " Betty Jean's mother knew something strange had happened to her daughter, but right then it was time to eat.[7]

It is all right to use the language of Zion to communicate with the children of Zion, but not with non-Christians who have no idea what church language means. Words and phrases like "born again," "walk down the aisle," "saved," "washed in the blood," "second coming," "brother," "sister," "beloved," "the invitation," and so forth may have great meaning for Christians; but to the uninitiated they may be so much sounding brass or tinkling cymbals.

The principle of uniqueness agrees with Arthur McPhee's paraphrase of 1 Corinthians 14:19, "I would rather speak five intelligible words to instruct others than ten thousand words in evangelicalese."[8] The use of in-house evangelical language when witnessing to outsiders violates the principle of uniqueness.

If we imitate the principle of uniqueness in our evangelism, we may have to give more attention to friendship evangelism. We really can't get to know just how unique a person is until we get to that individual. Our uniqueness is a many-faceted aspect of human personality. Like an iceberg, only the tip of one's uniqueness is seen at a glance. Most uniqueness lies below the surface. That's the reason Arthur McPhee thinks we usually try to share too much, too rich, too fast, and too foolish.[9]

Another way of putting this is to say, "Your greatest witness is your deepest relationship." That is the primary thesis of McPhee's book on *Friendship Evangelism.* "The best evangelism takes place in a context of mutual trust and respect," says McPhee. "It takes place between friends."[10]

Sociologists tell us that the normal sphere of human contacts is about twenty people. Those twenty persons constitute our immediate sphere of influence. They are what Tom Wolf calls our *oikos,* our household.[11] If we follow the principle of uniqueness, we shall seek to find the unique openings into their lives whereby Christ may enter and become a welcome guest.

The principle of uniqueness, when practiced, will give due attention to what might be called contextual evangelism. Evangelism never occurs in a cultural vacuum, but always in a particular cultural context. At least three cultural contexts are always present in all cross-cultural evangelism. There is the cultural context of the witness, that of the potential disciple, and that of the message. When we add to that the fact that there are perhaps six thousand cultures in the world, we dare not take lightly the need to contextualize our evangelism.

Those who take seriously the principle of uniqueness can better grasp the idea that "like reaches like" in evangelism. Women as a general rule can best reach unreached women. Men as a general rule can best reach unreached men. Youth as a general rule can best reach unreached youth. Those of one culture as a general rule can best reach the unreached of their own culture. Those of one profession as a general rule can best reach the unreached of that profession. Those of one homogeneous unit can as a general rule best reach the unreached of that homogeneous group. Those of one family can as a general rule best reach those of their family who are unreached.

Summary

We have looked at several examples from the evangelism of Jesus to show that this peerless Evangelist dealt with every person as a unique creation of God, that he had no stereotyped methods which were used with every person. I hope I have shown that this principle of uniqueness has numerous applications in our evangelism. Among those which I have lifted up are the following: different folk require different strokes; it keeps witness from degenerating into rigmarole; it means we can find a witnessing style which is natural for us; it points us to the need for a variety of witnessing methods and styles; it enables us to communicate more effectively by using a language which outsiders understand; it draws attention to the relational, contextual, and human nature of evangelism.

Other applications of the uniqueness principle may be made to what church growth theorists call the homogeneous unit principle and the receptivity principle. Moreover, it might be applied to help correct what the church growth people call the church growth disease of "people blindness."

Jesus did not deal with people the same way. He approached them by considering each person's uniqueness. Jesus is our example.

Notes

1. Henry Drummond, *The New Evangelism* (London: Hodder and Stoughton, 1899), p. 203.

2. Ken Anderson, *A Coward's Guide to Witnessing* (Carol Stream, Ill.: Creation House, 1972), p. 113.

3. Rebecca Manley Pippert, *Out of the Salt-Shaker & into the World* (Downers Grove, Illinois: Inter-Varsity Press, 1979), p. 124.

4. Ibid., pp. 9-13.

5. Quoted by George G. Hunter III, *The Contagious Congregation* (Nashville: Abingdon, 1979), p. 67.

6. See I. Wayan Mastra, "Contextualization of the Church in Bali: A Case Study from Indonesia," in John Stott and Robert T. Coote, eds., *Gospel & Culture* (Pasadena, Calif.: Wm. Carey Library, 1979), p. 363.

7. Trudy Horton, "Religious Jargon," *The Baptist Program*, February, 1980, p. 4.

8. Arthur McPhee, *Friendship Evangelism: The Caring Way to Share Your Faith* (Grand Rapids, Michigan: Zondervan Publishing House, 1978), p. 98.

9. Ibid., pp. 92-93.

10. Ibid., pp. 101.

11. Thomas A. Wolf, "Oikos Evangelism: Key to the Future," in Ralph Neighbour, compiler, *Future Church* (Nashville: Broadman Press, 1980), pp. 153-176.

5
Opportunism

Theme: Jesus seized every opportunity to bear witness
Scripture Lesson: Esther 4:13-14; Luke 19:1-10

Introduction

A fourth principle of evangelism according to Christ is what I call opportunism. Sometime, unwittingly, we assign a negative value judgment to that word. What I mean by it is that Jesus took advantage of every opportunity he had to share with people, and so should we. There was a kind of spontaneity about his witnessing. Often it was impromptu, "by the way" witnessing. It was unpremeditated. As Jesus passed by, an opportunity presented itself; he reached out and seized it.

Evangelism Where You Find It

Evangelism is where you find it. For Jesus it was as he sat down to rest beside a well in Samaria or as he was passing by and heard a blind man crying out, "Jesus, Son of David, have mercy on me" (Luke 18:38). Jesus seemed never to miss seeing any opportunity. J. H. Jowett says Jesus' eyes were like two eagle scouts. He saw Nathanael under the fig tree. He saw Matthew at the seat of custom. He saw that blind beggar beside the road outside Jericho. And he saw Zacchaeus up that sycamore tree.

L. R. Scarborough says of Jesus: "He was a mountain-side, way-side, well-side, open-air preacher."[1] Again in another place, Scarbough puts the same truth a different way: "He was a highway and a hedgeway preacher. He was a quiet seeker after souls."[2]

The case of Zacchaeus is a good one to demonstrate the principle of opportunism. Jesus was in a hurry to get to Jerusalem for his death. He had set his face like a flint toward the Holy City. He was in such haste that his disciples had some difficulty keeping up with him as they walked along the way. Nevertheless, when he entered into Jericho, he stopped right beneath that sycamore tree and looked up and saw Zacchaeus. Instantly, Jesus knew that here was a man who needed him. The journey to Jerusalem would have to wait. Jesus invited himself to dine with Zacchaeus. That was the best news he had heard since he sold his soul to the Roman government for the privilege of collecting taxes. Probably no self-respecting person had dined with Zacchaeus since he became a tax collector. His whole life was transformed that day because Jesus seized the opportunity to share with him.

If we pattern our evangelism after that of Jesus, we too will seize every opportunity which God gives us to share the word of life. Think of the normal, natural opportunities which God gives you at work, at recreation, at school, at home, in the organizations to which you belong. Remember, evangelism is where you find it.

Some of you have heard of Pastor Martin Niemoller of Germany who was imprisoned by Hitler for opposing Nazism. Niemoller was on the front page of *Time* magazine in May of 1940. The caption to Niemoller's picture read, "In Germany the cross has not bowed to the Swastika." That quotoation was prompted by the brave preacher and his famous sermon, "God Is My Fuhrer."

Niemoller, along with Karl Barth and Dietrich Bonhoeffer, helped form the Confessing Church and drew up the Barmen Declaration, one of the great theological documents of this century. Niemoller spent seven or eight years in Nazi jails. But it wasn't until several years into his imprisonment that Niemoller recognized his opportunity and responsibility to witness.

About the fourth year of his incarceration, Niemoller had a dream one night. In this dream, he saw Hitler standing before the judgment bar of God and pleading that he had never heard the gospel. Then, Niemoller says: "In my dream I heard the voice of God directed toward me inquiring, 'Were you with him one whole hour and did not tell him about my Son?' " When Niemoller awakened and reflected upon his dream, he remembered that he had, indeed, been with Adolph Hitler one whole hour and had said nothing to him about Jesus Christ. From that moment on, Pastor Niemoller began to seize every opportunity to witness to his guards and to those who came and went from his prison cell. That's the principle of opportunism.

Evangelism is where you find it. And sometime you find it in unexpected places.

One Sunday afternoon, during the last decade, I went out with a pastor to do some witness visitation in the homes of his community. One of our prospects lived at an address which we couldn't locate. It was in a semirural area. We stopped at a house to inquire about the directions.

To our surprise, the only person at that home was a young man in his early twenties who had recently been in a motorcycle accident. One of his legs was in a heavy cast, and he couldn't get around without crutches. He couldn't help us find the prospect for whom we were looking.

As we talked on, we discovered that the young man was not a Christian. In fact, he was hungry to hear the gospel.

We spent a wonderful hour with him and introduced him to the Savior. We never did find our original prospect. Nevertheless, I think we found the person to whom God had sent us. Don't you? That's practicing the principle of opportunism in evangelism.

Evangelism Is Where You Want to Find It

Evangelism is not just where you find it; it is more properly *wherever* you *want* to find it. David Watson illustrates this truth with an incident from his own ministry. Watson had gone on a vacation to Cornwall. This was before he was married and had any responsibility for children. He took along his books and had intended to converse with no one. His intention was to catch up on his reading while he rested in his hotel.

However, while praying one morning of that week, Watson felt God gently rebuking him for his silence. He came out of his room to the hotel lobby. It was a rainy day, and the guests were just lounging around looking out of the window and hoping it would soon clear up.

Sitting near Watson was a man about his age, whom he secretly envied for several days. This man appeared to have everything: a beautiful wife, two handsome children, a Charles Atlas body, an easy manner, and a prosperous business. The man was a kind of modern rich young ruler.

Very shortly Watson was in deep conversation with the man. They talked that day for three hours about the most basic issues of life and death, God, and humanity. The gentleman confessed that he had everything except an ultimate purpose in life.

Several conversations followed during the next few days. Then, the holiday ended. Two weeks later that man gave his life to Christ. Today, a good many years afterwards, God is doing a wonderful work in his life and in his family.[3]

All of that came about because Watson wanted to find an opportunity to witness. Had Watson not been willing to seize that opportunity, he would have never seen it.

During the American Civil War, a farmer was drafted into the Confederate Army. He didn't know how to drill or salute. Nor did the farmer know the various bugle calls. He brought his squirrel rifle with him. A command was given to attack and charge the Union forces. Off the farmer went with the Greys against the Blues. The bugle called retreat, but the farmer did not return. "Poor old Jim," his comrades said, "he was either killed or taken prisoner in the first battle he fought." However, when the sun started to go down, here came Jim. "It's Jim; it's Jim," they shouted, "and he's got a prisoner. Where did you get him, Jim?" they asked.

"Where did I get him," the farmer said, "the woods are full of them; why don't you get one yourself?"[4]

Sinners are, indeed, almost everywhere. Those who follow the principle of opportunism will find them and will be found by them. Evangelism is wherever you want to find it!

Redeeming the Time

Martin Buber, the Jewish philosopher and theologian, has unknowingly helped me to understand this principle of opportunism. Somewhere, in one of his books, Buber tells of a young man who came to see him one day. Buber was very busy and quickly rushed the young man out of his presence. The next day Buber read in the newspaper how that young man had committed suicide.

That incident impressed upon Buber the seriousness of time. It shocked him into the realization that every moment of time is pregnant with eternity. Buber determined never again to be too busy to seize an opportunity to counsel with a troubled person.

I believe that some opportunities never pass our way but once. Time is linear, not cyclical. That is the Judeo-Christian concept of time. We dare not believe that history always repeats itself.

The only time we have to evangelize our world is the NOW time. There is a certain "todayness" in the Bible which ought to encourage us to be more realistic about our opportunities to bear witness. "Today, when you hear his voice, do not harden your hearts" (Heb. 3:15). "This is the day which the Lord has made" (Ps. 118:24).

John R. Mott's great slogan, "The Evangelization of the World in This Generation," is still realistic because *this* is the only generation which we can evangelize. The principle of opportunism confronts us with the haunting question: If not now, then when? If we do not seize the natural, normal opportunities which God gives us to bear witness almost every day of our lives, when, if ever, will we?

Moreover, we should not think that the principle of opportunism has only to do with quantitative time. It also relates to qualitative time.

A word from the apostle Paul may throw some light on what is meant by the principle of opportunism. Toward the end of Colossians, Paul gave some instructions about Christian behavior toward unbelievers (Col. 4:5-6). The applicable phrase is, "making the most of the time" (v. 5). Some translate it, "redeeming the time" or "buying up the time."

One idea conveyed by such translations is that time is so precious that we are to use it as though we had to pay for every second of it. However true that may be, that is not quite what Paul had in mind.

There are two great Greek words for time. One is *chronos,* the root word from which we get our word *chronology. Chronos* time is chronological time, such as seconds, minutes, hours, days, weeks, months, years, and centuries. That is not the word Paul used in Colossians 4:5.

Rather, it is the word *kairos*. That is the other word for time. *Kairos* time is seasonal time, such as winter and summer, autumn and spring. It is crisis time, the time of divine appointment.

The Chinese word for crisis has a striking similarity to this Greek word *kairos*. It has two meanings and requires two Chinese characters. One character stands for peril or danger; the other for opportunity.

What Paul seems to have been saying is that there are "seasons of the soul" much as there are seasons of nature. Christians are to make the most of the time by watching for those most opportune seasons in the lives of lost persons and using those divinely appointed *kairoi* to bear witness to Jesus Christ.

We know that the passages from childhood into puberty and then from adolescence into adulthood appear to be natural seasons of the soul. And so with marriage, birth, sickness, and death. However, let us not stop just with seizing these divinely appointed opportunities for evangelizing. There may be one dozen or one hundred or more such *kairoi* in every person's life. Our business is to be so sensitive to these crises that we make the most of them for God. That is the principle of opportunism in operation. Such sensitivity to what is going on in the lives of our lost kinfolk, friends, and associates is possible only through caring and continuing relationships.

The principle of opportunism really does fit what is now being called life-style evangelism.[5] Lay people especially have many opportunities to share Christ these days. "Worldlings are looking for spiritual answers right where they are, in the sweat and smudge of life as they know it," says Ken Anderson, "and when they see someone relating faith to that kind of life, it registers."[6]

Conclusion

Yet, none of what we have said about the principle of opportunism should prevent us from seeking to create some opportunities for witnessing. Most of us are so constructed that we need the discipline of regular, scheduled visitation evangelism in the homes of the lost. When we covenant together with God and with one or two other Christians to go out witnessing at a certain time and place every week, that can better sensitize us to the normal opportunities which come our way in the course of our daily living.

Certainly, nothing should ever be said or done to put down those who systematically and faithfully go out to share their faith in an organized and structured manner. On the contrary, we ought to honor those who honor Christ in this way. Organized witnessing is not a hindrance to the principle of opportunism; it is a great help.

Goethe said people were meant to be hammers and not anvils. When we take the initiative in evangelizing the lost, we are being God's hammers and seeking to enable others to be hammers for God. Are you a hammer or an anvil? The principle of opportunism pulls us toward the hammer role.

Notes

1. L. R. Scarborough, *How Jesus Won Men* (Grand Rapids, Mich.: Baker Book House, 1972 reprint), p. 16.

2. L. R. Scarborough, *With Christ After the Lost* (New York: George H. Doran Co., 1919), p. 59.

3. David Watson, *I Believe in Evangelism* (Grand Rapids, Mich.: Wm. B. Eerdmans Publishing Co., 1976), pp. 100-101.

4. Related by John R. Rice, *The Soul Winner's Fire* (Wheaton, Illinois: The Sword of the Lord Publishers, 1941), p. 28.

5. See C. B. Hogue, *Love Leaves No Choice: Life-Style Evangelism* (Waco, Texas: Word Books, Publisher, 1976).

6. Ken Anderson, *A Coward's Guide to Witnessing* (Carol Stream, Ill.: Creation House, 1972), p. 105.

6
Sharing

Theme: Jesus gave himself and his mission to others
Scripture Lesson: Genesis 4:8-16; Matthew 25:31-46

Introduction

Sharing is a fifth principle of evangelism according to Christ. There was a kind of prodigality about the way Jesus shared with others. He gave himself with abandonment. Moreover, we see this principle operating in *what* he shared as well as in *how* he shared. Hence, both the style and the substance of his sharing are instructive.

His Example and Commission

Jesus gave his best to those whom many of his contemporaries judged the worst persons of his day: tax collectors, lepers, demoniacs, prostitutes, wine-bibbers, Samaritans, the lame, the halt, the blind, the sick, and the afflicted. The Gospel of Luke is so full of such examples that it has been labeled "The Gospel to the Outcasts."

Indeed, Luke begins the public ministry of Jesus with our Lord stating his mission in the words of Isaiah 61:1-2. He contended that he had been sent and anointed "to preach good news to the poor . . . to proclaim release to the captives and recovering of sight to the blind, to set at liberty those who are oppressed," and to announce the year of Jubilee (4:18-19).

The rest of Luke shows how Jesus fulfilled that mission. For example, only the Gospel of Luke relates the stories of the good Samaritan (10:29-31), of the lost coin and the lost prodigal (15:8-32), of Dives and Lazarus (16:19-31), and that of Zacchaeus (19:1-10).

Then, when we come to the Book of Acts, Luke continued to

show how the early church obeyed our Lord's commission to be witnesses in Jerusalem, Judea, Samaria, and to the end of the earth (1:8).
This sharing with outcasts which began in the Gospel of Luke is extended in Acts to "priests" (6:7), Samaritans (8:4 *ff.*), an Ethiopian
God-fearer who was also an eunuch (8:26 *ff.*), a Roman centurion and
his household (10—11), and eventually to many Gentiles in both Asia
and Europe (11—28). A "thirteenth" apostle, Saul of Tarsus, became
known as the "apostle to the Gentiles."

Hence our Lord set in motion, with his example and commission,
a sharing which eventually crossed all geographical and cultural bar-
riers. As Peter said of the church, "Once you were no people but now
you are God's people; once you had not received mercy but now you
have received mercy" (1 Pet. 2:10). We were named *Loammi* (No
People), but now we are named *Ammi* (People). We were *Loruhamah*
(No Mercy), but now we are *Ruhamah* (Mercy) (see Hos. 1:6 to 2:1,
23).

His Crucifixion

Lest we think our Lord's sharing was merely by example and only
in his commands and precepts, we should take a hard look at his death
on the cross. Jesus ultimately shared his very life's blood and his own
body on a cursed tree for us and for our salvation. Thus his sharing involved tears as well as talk, trials as well as triumphs, and sorrow and
suffering as well as joy and jubilation.

Paul put it this way: We Gentiles were the uncircumcision, "separated from Christ, alienated from the commonwealth of Israel, and
strangers to the covenants of promise, having no hope and without
God in the world. But now in Christ Jesus" we "who once were far off
have been brought near in the blood of Christ. For he is our peace,
who has made us both one, and has broken down the dividing wall of
hostility, by abolishing in his flesh the law of commandments and
ordinances, that he might create in himself one new man in place of
the two, so making peace . . . through the cross" (Eph. 2:11-16).

This principle of sharing says something about Jesus' caring and
ours. Remember the explanation of a CARE package: "If we care . . .

we share"? "It is a fact that if we care enough," says John Havlik, "we will find a way to share."[1] Our problem in sharing is not so much the "how" as it is that we have not been grasped by the "why." God so loved that he found a way to share. When we so love, we will also find a way to share.

Two Grand Aspects to His Sharing

It appears from what has been said thus far about the principle of sharing that there were two grand aspects to its operation in the evangelism of Jesus. First, Jesus shared the best that he had with some of the most notorious persons of his time. For example, he preached one of his greatest sermons to the Samaritan prostitute at Jacob's well (see John 4:4-42). What a shame, some might think, to waste such beautiful words on a solitary, half-breed who was the town tart!

Well, Jesus did not think it a waste. Nor did he see only the dark side of this woman's life. And what a harvest of precious souls our Lord reaped in Sychar because he shared the best that he had with one of the most notorious women in that city (see John 4:39-41).

About the same thing may be observed in our Lord's dealings with Zacchaeus (Luke 19:1-10), the woman taken in the very act of adultery (John 8:3-11), the Gerasene demoniac (Mark 5:1-20), the rich young ruler (Mark 10:17-22), and the man blind from birth (John 9:1 *ff.*). Each of these was only one person. They were either down-and-out or up-and-out. Many looked down upon them. Some even despised them. Yet our Lord loved them and gave himself to them and for them. He spent time with them and gave them the best which he had to offer. Is it any wonder that most of them were transformed and became new creations?

I have noticed a tendency in my ministry to want to share the best that I have with the best and with the most. Somehow I have wanted to save my best sermons for the best and biggest congregations, my best lectures for the brightest and biggest classes, my best thoughts for the best individuals and for the most alert groups with which I deal. Not so, Jesus. He shared his best with individuals, even with some of the worst persons in his society.

If we would learn from Jesus to share our best—our best selves and our best ideas, our best time and our best gifts—with those whom many consider to be the worst folk in our day, we too might see some miraculous changes occur in their lives as happened in the days of our Lord's flesh. Perhaps we too should learn to give ourselves with prodigality to the dropouts, cop-outs, and cast outs of our society.

Could it still be true after all these centuries that "the tax collectors and the harlots go into the kingdom of God" (see Matt. 21:31) before the respectable sinners? One way for us to find out for sure is to give our best to them as did our Lord.

A second grand aspect which we may observe in our Lord's application of this sharing principle is that he even shared his mission with his disciples. Jesus didn't try to do all of the witnessing alone. The Johannine form of the Great Commission says, "As the Father has sent me, even so I send you" (John 20:21).

That fits what Jesus had said in John 14:12, "Truly, truly, I say to you, he who believes in me will also do the works that I do; and greater works than these will he do, because I go to the Father." We Christians are an extension of Christ's incarnation. The church as the continuing body of Christ in the world does the same works which Jesus did in the days of his flesh. By "greater works" he means more, not more spectacular, but more in number and quantity because the disciples are at it over a much longer time span than was he.

This same form of the Great Commission in John's Gospel gives us a clue as to how it is that we can share in our Lord's mission to the world. The risen Christ also shares the Holy Spirit with those who are to share in his mission. Note how in conjunction with the commissioning words, our Lord breathed on them and said: "Receive the Holy Spirit. If you forgive the sins of any, they are forgiven; if you retain the sins of any, they are retained" (John 20:22-23).

Hence, that "all authority" which has been given to Jesus in the Matthean form of the Great Commission (see Matt. 28:18) is shared with the disciples. To state it a bit differently, the promise, "lo, I am with you always, to the close of the age" (see Matt. 28:20), is literally fulfilled in the presence and the power of the Holy Spirit which God has given to the church (see Acts 1—2).

Therefore, Christ shares his mission and gives us the power of his Spirit to engage in that mission. When he began his public ministry, one of the first things Jesus did was to call twelve to be with him. He shared all that the twelve were able to receive from him during his public ministry. The rest he trusted the Holy Spirit to convey to them after he had ascended (see John 16:12-15).

This is a vital aspect of our Lord's sharing which you and I need to imitate today. None of us can do all of the witnessing which needs to be done in the world. There are not enough ordained preachers, missionaries, and other full-time Christian workers in the whole church to do all of the evangelizing which is mandated by our Lord. We need to learn to share our Lord's mission with all of the disciples.

So long as memory serves me, I think I shall never forget the tearful words of a pastor who said to me as he was about to retire from the active pastorate:

If I had my ministry to live over, I would seek more diligently to equip others to share their faith. Most of my ministry I have myself won most of the persons to Christ whom I have baptized. It ought not to be that way, but now it's too late for me to start over.

One of the truly hopeful signs in today's church is the increasing number of church leaders who are beginning to see themselves as equippers of others. Nevertheless, professional church leaders are not the only ones who need to share the mission of our Lord with others. Every member of the body of Christ needs to share in this mission with all other members of the body. Only as each Christian in every place, in his or her particular vineyard, shares his or her part of that mission can it be accomplished.

The task of world evangelization is impossible apart from this aspect of sharing. But if each of us will share his or her part of the responsibility, we can become co-laborers together with Christ in world redemption.

Sharing Ourselves

This principle of sharing, when applied to evangelism, runs so deeply that it goes far beyond the sharing of our best with the worst and our sharing the mission of Christ with all other Christians. If we pattern our evangelism after our Lord's, it involves nothing less than the sharing of ourselves with others.

The Macedonian Christians did not have much material wealth to give. Nevertheless, "first they gave themselves to the Lord" (2 Cor. 8:5). Then out of their extreme poverty, they overflowed in a wealth of liberality toward the poor Christians in Jerusalem! As Elizabeth Seton put it, they were willing to "live simply that others may simply live."

A·letter to the editor of the *Christian Century* spoke of the more than 125,000 Cuban and Haitian refugees who had arrived on the shores of Miami, Florida. The writer said:

We've found that, more than sharing material possessions, there is a need to share ourselves, emotionally and spiritually, with these new neighbors.

It takes all our time, all our strength, all our sensitivity. But then, where else could these be better expended?[2]

What I mean by sharing ourselves is the exact opposite of selfishness and narcissism which so pervade our culture today. Do you recall the poem about Narcissus, the Greek god who fell in love with his own reflection?

> There once was a nymph named Narcissus
> Who thought himself very delicious
> So he stared like a fool
> At his face in a pool
> And his folly today is still with us.[3]

I like the two questions which a Christian dentist put to himself while practicing in Jackson, Mississippi: "What difference would one less dentist make in Jackson, Mississippi?" *versus* "What difference could one more dentist make in the Ivory Coast, a country with more than seven million people and only seven or eight dentists all the time?" Answering those questions took Charles and Dianne Deevers to Bouaké, Ivory Coast, as missionaries. Dr. Deevers now sees an average of sixty patients a day. Whereas, in this country twenty per day would have been considered a heavy case load. Moreover, at least half of the sixty to eighty Africans who attend worship services at the mission church in Bouaké have come as a direct result of the ministry of the dental clinic which Dr. Deevers directs.[4]

Applying the principle of sharing to world evangelization may give us more servants like Charles and Dianne Deevers. If more of us would give ourselves like the Deevers, we might multiply beautiful stories in our time like that of Albrecht Dürer and the Praying Hands from a previous age. You will recall that Dürer dreamed of becoming a painter. He had no money. Going to Nuremberg, Germany, he lived with an older man who also was poor. It was decided that one would work and the other would study. The older man insisted that Dürer go to school while he worked at hard labor. Later the older man discovered that toil had so stiffened and gnarled his hands that he could never paint. Dürer was filled with sorrow upon learning of what had happened. One day he entered the room and saw his friend with reverently folded hands in prayer. In appreciation, he painted those folded hands. They remain a symbol of unselfish service and noble character.

Sharing Our Material Wealth

Sharing does relate to material wealth as well as to ourselves. NBC's "Today Show" reported on August 11, 1980, that there are thirty thousand homeless persons in New York City. These people sleep on the streets, in the parks, or wherever they can find a place.

There are homeless persons in almost every city of our country. Larry Rice of the New Life Evangelistic Center in Saint Louis says there are five thousand in that city. "These are the American refugees that no one helps," says Rice; "they can't even get welfare because they don't have a permanent address."[5]

Ron Sider has suggested that we are living in an age of hunger. Sider has called on rich Christians to share what they have with those who have not. He believes if only one tenth of us Christians in the rich nations dared to join hands with the poor of the earth and began to live out the implications of the gospel, we would change the course of history.

Sider sees particular irony in the fact that those of us who claim to be most biblical seem to prefer to teach Romans and to neglect the message of Amos. We believe the entire canon to be fully inspired, but we hedge on the theme of economic justice.

Could it be that there really is a close connection between our sharing with the poor and our evangelism? Sider goes so far as to say:

The present division between haves and have-nots in the body of Christ terribly hinders world evangelism. Hungry people find it difficult to accept a Christ preached by people who symbolize (and often defind the affluence of) the earth's richest society.[6]

Ask yourself these five questions: Do I have food for at least three meals on hand? Do I have clothes to wear? Do I have shelter over my head? Do I have some means of transportation? Do I have a job which remunerates me for my labor? If so, you are in the top 1 percent of the world's population! Now ask yourself: From where did I get all of these things? Did they not come from the hands of God? Should I not praise and thank God for these material blessings? If for no other reason but gratitude for what God has done for us, we ought to give back to God a part of that which has has given to us. The tithe is a symbol of our gratitude to God.

When Jesus said, "Render to Caesar the things that are Caesar's, and to God the things that are God's" (see Mark 12:17), he was saying "give back to Caesar and to God the things which are their's." The emphasis is upon what we have *received* and not upon what we *give*.

"We are a nation of consumerholics," says Henlee Barnette. We Americans have 6 percent of the world's population, yet we consume about 40 percent of the world's resources. The rising cost of materials which we secure from the Third World nations may force us to consume less in the years to come.[7]

An old Paraguayan proverb says, "No one listens to the cry of the poor or the sound of a wooden bell." The sound of a wooden bell couldn't be heard very far. But why can we not hear the cry of the poor? Is it because they are too weak and powerless? One ministry of the church might be to amplify the cry of the poor. Yet, how shall we magnify that cry when we are too insensitive to hear it ourselves?

The Africans have a way of expressing things in proverbs and distilled wisdom. For example, one of their greetings has the first person say, "Are you well?"

Then, the second person replies, "I am if you are." None of us is ever truly well unless the others are. We are all part of a corporate bundle of life. This is especially true of us who constitute the beloved community of the church. We are our brother's keeper.

Sharing as a Law of Supply

Apparently there is what might be called a law of supply in sharing. Love's arithmetic is always in the red. We can never repay the debts we owe to God and to others.

> If I have fire, I owe the world some heat,
> If I have food, I owe the world some meat,
> If I have melody, I owe the world a song,
> If I have peace, I owe the world no wrong.
> Author Unknown

Remember what happened to the manna in the wilderness? If the Israelites tried to save it from one day until the next, except for the sabbath day, it would rot. God's blessings are given in order that they might be shared. Try to save up some of your blessings, and they will rot. Share them and you cast your bread upon the waters.

D. W. Flint, one of Henry Ford's early associates, was asked by Ford one day what his chief ambition in life was. "To make a million dollars and then to take life easy," was Flint's quick reply.

Several days later, Ford walked into Flint's office and laid a package on his desk. "It's for you. Open it," Ford said. The package contained a pair of rimmed eyeglasses from which the lenses had been removed and two round silver dollars substituted.

"Put them on," Ford insisted. "Now what do you see? "I see nothing," said Flint. "How can I? The dollars get in the way."

"You get the message," Ford said with a grin. "Make dollars your objective, see nothing but money, and the dollars will, indeed, get in your way. But if you forget the dollars and focus on giving rather than getting and really render service, the dollars will take care of themselves. Practice the law of supply."

Ford explained the law of supply to his mystified friend. Giving activates good by stimulating the free flow of values. On the basis of this law, you don't get by grabbing but by giving.[8]

John Wesley practiced this law of supply. When he died in his eighty-eighth year on March 12, 1791, Wesley left behind one silver spoon, a worn-out clergyman's coat, and a badly abused reputation. However, he also left the world the Methodist Church.

Maxey Jarman, a well-known Christian businessman who died in 1980, gave very generously to the Lord's work. Once when he had taken some large losses in business, a friend asked him, "Maxey, haven't you ever regretted the money you gave to Christian causes?"

Mr. Jarman replied, "The way I see it, the only money I didn't lose was what I gave!"[9]

Dom Helder Camara, a Roman Catholic archbishop of Brazil, has been quoted as saying: "Poverty makes people subhuman. Excess of wealth makes people inhuman." So, both the poor and the rich have problems. Perhaps if more of us practiced the law of supply, that might prevent us from becoming inhuman and keep others from becoming subhuman.

Sharing Our Love and Care

It isn't just money and material possessions and the content of the gospel which we need to share with others. We need to learn to share our love. A divorcee who had dropped out of the church said if she were going to say only one thing to the church, it would be, "Love me!"[10] The gospel is not just good news at the beginning of the Christian life. It is good news at the beginning and the ending and all along the way. Love is meeting human needs. It is willing to forgive "seventy times seven" and to love in spite of everything.

I saw where a Presbyterian church advertised itself in *Christianity Today* as "The church where the people care." Not bad if true! We know God cares for us. Psalm 8:4 says, "What is man that thou art mindful of him, and the son of man that thou dost care for him?" We are even admonished in 1 Peter 5:7, "Cast all your anxieties on him, for he cares about you."

The Bible also speaks of shepherds who are to care for the people (see Jer. 23:1-4). Surely, we expect men and women who are set apart as God's undershepherds to care for us. But a church—a whole community of Christians—where the people care, that is a rare jewel in many places on this planet.

Yet, why should that kind of caring fellowship not be the rule rather than the exception? Are we not all either shepherds or lambs? Should not every Christian be a shepherd to some lamb(s)? I like what I read about the Episcopal church which seeks to conserve its evangelistic harvest by assigning a shepherd member to every new lamb who enters its fold. Such a church can truthfully fly a banner which reads: "The church where the people care."

That question which a popular Christian song raises, "Do you really care?" is an appropriate one for us to put to ourselves and to our churches. Is it nothing to us that more than 3 billion of the world's citizens are "dead in trespasses and sins" and do not know that they can find in Jesus Christ the Bread of life? Is it nothing to us that there are perhaps up to 16,750 hidden people groups scattered throughout the world and among whom is no church? Is it nothing to us that so many people of our planet have a multitude of elemental needs which so few care so little about?

Conclusion

"Do you really care?" Do we care for those who care for us? Do we care *only* for those who care for us? Do we care for those who don't care for themselves, for others, or for God? Do we care with *agape* love? Do we care enough to become a new kind of incarnation among them?

Do we care enough to share our best with the worst? Do we care enough to share our Lord's mission with all of God's people? Do we care enough to share ourselves, our material wealth, our friendship, and our love?

The principle of sharing in evangelism teaches us that Jesus gave himself away. "Truly, truly, I say to you, unless a grain of wheat falls into the earth and dies, it remains alone; but if it dies, it bears much fruit" (John 12:24). Furthermore, "He who finds his life will lose it, and he who loses his life for my sake will find it" (Matt. 10:39). Only as we give ourselves and our mission to others can we model our evangelism after his.

We need to be constantly evangelized ourselves. The good news needs to be proclaimed in our midst. The call to kingdom life must be issued daily. Our effectiveness as proclaimers of the kingdom will be no greater than the degree to which Christ is formed within us.

Notes

1. John F. Havlik, "A Theology for An Evangelistic Church," *Church Administration*, Vol. 21, No. 9, June, 1979, p. 3.

2. See *The Christian Century*, Vol. XCVII, No. 26, August 13-20, 1980, p. 805, the letter by Charles A. Robertson.

3. Quoted by John Piper in *Christianity Today*, Vol. XXI, No. 21, Aug. 12, 1977, p. 6.

4. Baptist Press release, "He's Taking a Little Cut in Pay," *Baptist Courier*, Vol. 112, No. 39, Oct. 2, 1980, p. 2.

5. Quoted by Ed. Schafer, "300 Homeless Form Tent City in St. Louis Park," *The Kansas City Star*, Aug. 5, 1980, p. 4-A.

6. Ron Sider, "Christian Lifestyles in An Age of Hunger," *Home Missions*, Vol. 51, No. 6, Nov.-Dec., 1980, p. 38. See also pp. 37-40.

7. Henlee Barnette, "Stewardship of the Environment," *Light*, Oct.-Nov., 1980, p. 6. *Light* is a publication of the Christian Life Commission of the Southern Baptist Convention.

8. Related by Norman Vincent Peale, "You Can Reap More Than You Sow," *The Kansas City Star*, Mar. 1, 1980, p. 6-C.

9. Cited by Leighton Ford in his December, 1980, letter from the Lausanne Committee for World Evangelization.

10. See Margaret McCommon, "The Divorcee," *Home Missions*, Vol. 51, No. 6, Nov.-Dec., 1980, p. 52.

7
Dependency

Theme: Jesus exhibited a strong dependency upon the Holy Spirit
Scripture Lesson: Zechariah 4:6; Luke 11:14-26

Introduction

Evangelism is spiritual work which requires spiritual persons who have spiritual power. Whatever else Paul may have meant when he exhorted Timothy to "do the work of an evangelist" (2 Tim. 4:5), he was referring to spiritual work which is qualitatively different than merely selling life insurance. I should be surprised if a good insurance sales person couldn't apply many of his or her techniques to evangelistic ministry. However, the work of an evangelist is inseparably tied to the work of God's Spirit.

Moreover, the work of evangelism requires spiritual persons, that is persons upon whom the Holy Spirit has blown, brooded, brought into newness of life, and baptized with the fire of *agape* love. By spiritual persons I do not mean other-worldly persons entirely. Rather, I mean holy persons whose lives are characterized by a transcendent and godly dimension right in the midst of the hustle and bustle of daily existence. The spiritual person is one who walks in the Spirit and who lives under the control of the Holy Spirit.

Furthermore, the work of evangelism requires spiritual power. There is a superhuman dimension to evangelism which requires superhuman help. "Even the Lord of glory must have an enduement of the Spirit for his mission," exclaimed John Havlik. "Can we afford to go in the weakness of human activity, hoping that the arm of flesh will defeat the powers of hell?"[1]

The arm of flesh will inevitably fail us in the work of evangelism.

I find myself in agreement with Henry Drummond, "If miracle ceased with the first century, our faith, to a large extent, ceases with it."[2]

Jesus was the perfect spiritual Person who modeled for us this spiritual work of evangelism in the power of the Holy Spirit. Jesus in his matchless modeling of disciple-making exhibited and taught a strong dependency upon the Holy Spirit. That is a sixth great principle of evangelism according to Christ.

The Example of Jesus

Jesus never made a disciple, preached a sermon, or worked a miracle until the Holy Spirit came upon him at his baptism. As a matter of fact, from start to finish, the Spirit is connected with the life and ministry of Jesus. To begin with, he was conceived by the Holy Spirit in Mary's womb. The Scriptures say, "She was found to be with child of the Holy Spirit" (Matt. 1:18). Even Elizabeth, while yet pregnant with John the Baptist, was "filled with the Holy Spirit" (Luke 1:41). When the forerunner of Jesus was born, his father Zachariah was also "filled with the Holy Spirit" (Luke 1:67). Simeon, righteous and devout, was inspired by the Holy Spirit to welcome the child Jesus when his parents brought him to the Temple (see Luke 2:25-35).

The Holy Spirit descended on Jesus at his baptism. Luke says, "the Holy Spirit descended upon him in bodily form, as a dove, and a voice came from heaven, 'Thou art my beloved Son; with thee I am well pleased' " (3:22). John the Baptist said, "I saw the Spirit descend as a dove from heaven, and it *remained* on him" (John 1:32, *author's italics*.) I underscore that word *remained* because it suggests to us the possibility that the Spirit never left him during his earthly life and ministry.

Then, Luke continues to bracket our Lord's ministry with references to the Spirit. Luke 4:1-2 reads, "Jesus, full of the Holy Spirit, returned from the Jordan, and was led by the Spirit for forty days in the wilderness, tempted by the devil." Following the temptation of Jesus, Luke 4:14 begins, "Jesus returned in the power of the Spirit into Galilee."

Mark's Gospel uses an even stronger word than Luke or Matthew to describe the Spirit's role in the temptation of Jesus. "The Spirit immediately drove him out into the wilderness" (Mark 1:12). That word translated "drove" means "to drive him out" much as you and I would throw out a ball.

We see another glimpse into our Lord's dependency upon the Spirit in the discussion about casting out demons (see Luke 11:14-26). Jesus was accused of exorcising demons by the power of Beelzebul, the prince of demons. Our Lord made several points in reply to that ridiculous charge.

First, Jesus replied in effect, "If I cast out demons by the prince of demons, then Satan's kingdom is divided against itself! Surely no kingdom can stand in which the ruler lays waste his own kingdom" (see Luke 11:17-18).

Second, Jesus queried them, "If I cast out demons by Beelzebul, by whom do your sons cast them out?" (Luke 11:19). The implication is that since both he and they are casting out demons, how can his accusers know that their children are not also using the power of Beelzebul?

A third point made by our Lord is that no one can plunder a strong man's house unless that one is stronger (see Luke 11:21-23). Still, a fourth point is that unclean spirits have to be replaced with clean spirits or else one's last state is worse than the first (see Luke 11:24-26).

However, all of that is peripheral to the words of Jesus in Luke 11:20, "But if it is by the finger of God that I cast out demons, then the kingdom of God has come upon you." By "the finger of God" is meant the Spirit of God. Matthew 12:28 is an exact parallel which reads, "But if it is by the Spirit of God."

Therefore, Jesus claimed to do his exorcisms by the power of the Holy Spirit. The casting out of demons by Jesus were and are signs of the presence and the power of the kingdom of God. That is part of the reason Origen said Jesus was the *autobasileia*, or the kingdom in person.[3]

Make no mistake about it. Jesus was claiming to lay waste to the kingdom of Satan by the power of the Holy Spirit. He was implying that all evil spirits are cast out by the Holy Spirit. He was claiming that the power which he has is greater than the demonic powers. Indeed, he may have been claiming that when he cast out unclean spirits, he replaced them with the clean spirit of the Holy Spirit, who not only puts a house in order but is able to keep it in order.

I have been mostly following Luke's Gospel to show how Jesus exhibited his dependency upon the Holy Spirit in his life and ministry. Now, go with me to the end of that Gospel. There is the Lukan form of the Great Commission given by the risen Christ (see Luke 24:44-49). The last part of that commission says, "And behold, I send the promise of my Father upon you; but stay in the city, until you are clothed with power from on high" (Luke 24:49).

The second volume of the Luke-Acts narrative leaves no doubt but that "the promise of the Father" (compare Acts 1:4 with Luke 24:49) is the baptism of the Holy Spirit, and that "the power from on high" is the dynamite of the Spirit (see Acts 1:8). That baptism came at Pentecost; the fire fell and the waiting disciples were filled with power to carry on the work which our Lord began in the days of his flesh (see Acts 2:1-47). No wonder Acts is by some called "the Acts of the Holy Spirit."

Not only did Jesus exhibit a strong dependency upon the Holy Spirit but also he exhorted his disciples to exhibit and to teach that same dependency. That is the principle of dependency in our Lord's evangelism.

How did Luke account for the boldness and the vitality of the early church? "When they had prayed, the place in which they were gathered together was shaken; and they were all filled with the Holy Spirit and spoke the word of God with boldness" (Acts 4:31). These early Christians patterned their evangelizing after *The Jesus Model*.[4] They practiced the principle of dependency.

Other Aspects of Our Lord's Dependency

Apart from the above clear example and teachings of Jesus, we may point to several other evidences of our Lord's dependency. Jesus was a praying man. It was his habit to pray. He lived his earthly life in an attitude of prayer.

To pray is to confess that we are inadequate. To pray is to confess that God is adequate. As A. J. Gordon said, "We may do much after we have prayed."

Jesus prayed for others, as well as for himself. Prayer for others indicates that we are all dependent upon God. Perhaps to some extent, it also shows our dependency upon others.

"There is nothing that makes us love a man so much," says William Law, "as praying for him." Those who are serious about establishing a devout and holy life must learn how to pray. Likewise, those who would love others will learn to pray for them. Once I received a letter from a friend which began, "Dear Prayed for Delos." That was another way of saying, "Dear Loved Delos."

One of the sobering facts about the Model Prayer, which we call our Lord's Prayer, is that it shows both our dependency upon God and upon others. There is no trace of "rugged individualism" in the pattern prayer. As someone has written:

> You cannot say the Lord's Prayer
> and ever once say "I."
> You cannot pray the Lord's Prayer
> and ever once say "my."
> For others are included
> In each and every plea.
> From the beginning to the end of it,
> It does not once say "me."
> Anonymous

Jesus was also dependent upon others for his physical and material needs, voluntarily so to be sure. He could have turned the stones into bread. Instead he chose to let others furnish the bread or to do without. "Seek first his kingdom and his righteousness, and all these things shall be yours as well" (Matt. 6:33).

The one whom they called "the Savior of the world" (John 4:42) asked the Samaritan woman for a drink of water (John 4:7). He who called himself "the Son of man" (Luke 19:10) invited himself to be the guest of Zacchaeus. He depended upon others for water to quench his thirst and for food to nourish his body.

It may be well that you and I are dependent upon others for our physical and financial needs. Just that much dependency may drive us toward a greater dependency upon God's Spirit.

In chapter 3, I discussed the self-emptying of Jesus in the incarnation. Suffice it to say here that we may also see the dependency of Jesus in his babyhood, childhood, and teens. Have any of us fully plumbed the depths of those words: "Jesus increased in wisdom and stature, and in favor with God and man" (Luke 2:52)?

One more evidence of our Lord's dependency upon the Spirit may be seen in an imaginary conversation between Jesus and Gabriel. The legend is told that when Jesus returned to heaven he was asked by the angel Gabriel what plans were made to carry on his work. "Well, I have given the gospel to Peter and Mary and the others," he said. "They will pass it on."

"But suppose Peter gets too busy with his fishing, and Mary too occupied with her housework, and the others too concerned with their business, and they forget to pass the word along," the angel replied. "What plans have you then to reach the world with the good news?"

There was a moment of pause. Then with confidence in his voice, Jesus turned to Gabriel and said, "I have no other plans. I am counting on them!"[5]

Perhaps enough has been said to convince us of the principle's application in the evangelism of Jesus. More important now is the question of how the principle works in our evangelizing. Let me suggest several ways in which we are dependent upon the Holy Spirit.

The Holy Spirit Energizes

We are dependent upon the Holy Spirit to energize us to witness. He empowers us, according to Acts 1:8. Luke 24:49 uses the picturesque phrase, "clothed with power from on high."

That word for power is *dunamis,* the Greek word from which we get our English word *dynamite.* Jesus promised his disciples that they will be clothed with dynamite in order that they may be effective witnesses to him. We read, or hear, occasionally of a guerrilla warrior or a criminal taking an explosive charge into some crowded place. According to Jesus, his witnesses are clothed with dynamite, the dynamite of the Holy Spirit. They carry dynamite with them wherever they go. They are baptized, saturated, clothed, outfitted with the Holy Spirit.

God never intended that we should witness in our own strength. In the Great Commission of Matthew's Gospel, Jesus said, "Lo, I am with you always, to the close of the age" (Matt. 28:20). And he is with us through the Holy Spirit. What the Lord said to Zerubbabel, he says to us all: "Not by might, nor by power, but by my Spirit, says the Lord of hosts" (Zech. 4:6). It is not by artificial might or human power but by the power of God's Spirit that we are energized to bear witness to the Son of God.

The Holy Spirit Convicts

We are dependent upon the Holy Spirit in evangelism to convict the world of sin, of righteousness, and of judgment. John 16:8-11 reads:

> When he comes, he will convince the world of sin and of righteousness and of judgment; of sin, because they do not believe in me; of righteousness, because I go to the Father, and you will see me no more; of judgment, because the ruler of this world is judged.

This is what we mean by the old phrase "under conviction." Some persons are under conviction and some are not. All of those under conviction are convinced by the Holy Spirit. You and I can't convince anyone of sin. That is not our business. We are to bear witness to Jesus Christ. The Holy Spirit does the convicting.

This is also called "the office work of the Holy Spirit" by some of the older commentators. My office work is that of faithful witness bearing. I can't convince anyone by my clever phrases or by my overpowering arguments. If the Holy Spirit doesn't convict of sin, I can't.

Blasphemy against the Holy Spirit is the unpardonable sin because it is the Holy Spirit's work to convince persons of sin. If persons get so twisted and warped in their values and judgments that they attribute to Satan the work of God and to God the work of Satan, there is no hope for them. How can the Spirit convict someone of sin if he or she throws up that kind of roadblock? Blasphemy against the

Holy Spirit is unforgivable because the unbeliever acknowledges no sin to be forgiven (see Matt. 12:22-32; Mark 3:20-30; Luke 11:14-23; 12:10).

The Holy Spirit Regenerates

We are dependent upon the Holy Spirit to regenerate the lost. He effects the new birth. He brings new life to the one who is dead in trespasses and in sins. He raises those who are dead in sin.

The same Holy Spirit who was active in the old creation is active in the new creation. Those who are in Christ are new creations (see 2 Cor. 5:17), but they are made new creations through the work of the Holy Spirit. Jesus told Nicodemus, "Unless one is born of water and the Spirit, he cannot enter the kingdom of God" (John 3:5).

The new birth is after the analogy of the creation. Just as the Spirit of God brooded upon the primeval chaos of darkness, which was without form and void (see Gen. 1:2), so that same Spirit of God broods over every person who is dead in the darkness of sin, without God and without hope. He who brought order out of primeval chaos in the birth of the world, brings order out of chaos in the birth of a Christian.

The new birth is also after the analogy of the virgin birth of our Lord. Just as that which was conceived in the womb of the virgin Mary was the work of God's Spirit, so when one is conceived and born into the family of God, it is the work of the Holy Spirit.

The Holy Spirit Equips

We are dependent upon the Holy Spirit to equip the church with spiritual gifts for building up the body of Christ. The list of those gifts in Ephesians 4 includes evangelists, "His gifts were that some should be apostles, some prophets, some evangelists, some pastors and teachers, to equip the saints for the work of ministry, for building up the body of Christ" (Eph. 4:11-12).

The church is a Spirit-filled community. She is a gifted fellowship. The Holy Spirit has equipped her with those spiritual gifts which she needs to present every person mature in Christ. One of those gifts is evangelists.

I think we should readily acknowledge that some Christians seem to be gifted in evangelism above other Christians. For example, an arch-deacon who is now a bishop told me of an Episcopalian layman who has introduced ninety-four persons to Christ one by one during his lifetime and seen them all confirmed as members of local churches. The arch-deacon indicated that unfortunately no one else in his diocese had come anywhere close to ninety-four converts.

Nevertheless, it should be remembered that in Ephesians 4, all of the gifts are intended to equip the saints for the work of ministry, for building up the one body of Christ. So body building, and in this case the body is the whole church, is the purpose of every spiritual gift.

Those who call themselves charismatic today because they speak in tongues are not the only charismatics because all evangelism is charismatic. Evangelism is a charismatic work.

The Holy Spirit Inspires

We are dependent upon the Holy Spirit in evangelism to inspire us with what we are to say. It seems to me that the Spirit helps us with what we are to say in three ways. First, the Holy Spirit helps us with what we are to say by inspiring the Scriptures. Second, the Holy Spirit inspires what we are to say by, at times, giving us the very words and thoughts which we are to utter. Third, the Holy Spirit inspires us with what we are to say in preaching. Let us examine these three ideas more closely.

Paul wrote to Timothy, "All scripture is inspired by God" (2 Tim. 3:16). That is to say, all Scripture is God in-breathed. By what breath? The breath of God's Spirit. Jesus said in John's Gospel, "You search the scriptures, because you think that in them you have eternal life; and it is they that bear witness to me" (John 5:39).

The Bible is full of Christ. It is inspired truth which points us to him who is the Way, the Truth, and the Life. The Holy Spirit helps us with what we are to say in our evangelizing by giving us an inspired

Bible. This is the reason we use the Bible in seeking to convert lost persons to Jesus Christ.

Not only does the Holy Spirit give us the inspired Scriptures to use in our witnessing, he at times gives us the very words and thoughts we are to use (see Matt. 10:17-20). Sometimes we get uptight about what we will say if we are put on the spot. But I believe those who do their best to learn how to share their faith, and who try diligently to be prepared with what they will say, can always claim this promise. Brothers and sisters, "what you are to say will be given to you in that hour" by the Holy Spirit (see Matt. 10:19-20).

There is also a third way that the Holy Spirit inspires us with what we are to say in our evangelism. He helps us with our preaching. True preaching is what the Bible calls prophecy. And prophecy in the Bible—especially in the New Testament—is not so much foretelling the future as forthtelling God's will for the present.

That public proclamation of Jesus Christ which we call preaching is, at its best, inspired utterance which the Holy Spirit gives to the church through today's apostles, prophets, evangelists, pastors and teachers (see Eph. 4:11). The Holy Spirit inspires us in our evangelism by helping us with what we are to say in our preaching.

The Holy Spirit Guides

The Holy Spirit often guides us in our evangelism. That is another way in which we are dependent upon him. He frequently guides us to those to whom we are to witness. An excellent New Testament example of this is the way Philip was led to the Ethiopian eunuch. "An angel of the Lord said to Philip, 'Rise and go toward the south to the road that goes down from Jerusalem to Gaza.'. . . . And the Spirit said to Philip, 'Go up and join this chariot.'. . . . And when they came up out of the water, the Spirit of the Lord caught up Philip" (Acts 8:26,29,39). See how the Holy Spirit led Philip, the evangelist, to introduce this high official of Ethiopia to Christ?

One of the most remarkable passages in the Bible about how the Holy Spirit leads Christian workers to those persons and places where they are to evangelize is Acts 16:6-10. That same Spirit still leads us today.

Conclusion

The better definitions of evangelism always make some reference to the role of the Holy Spirit in evangelism. For example, the often quoted Anglican definition of 1918 and 1943 says:

To evangelize is so to present Christ Jesus in the power of the Holy Spirit, that men shall come to put their trust in God through Him, to accept Him as their Saviour, and serve Him as their King in the fellowship of His church.[6]

Note the phrase: "in the power of the Holy Spirit."

Such phrases are included in definitions because of the principle of dependency in evangelization. Evangelism worth its salt is always trinitarian and cannot be effective apart from the power of the Spirit of God. If Jesus, the Son of God, was dependent upon the Holy Spirit in his making of disciples, how much more should you and I be?

Notes

1. John F. Havlik, *Where in the World Is Jesus Christ?* (Nashville: Broadman Press, 1980), p. 47.

2. Henry Drummond, *The New Evangelism* (London: Hodder and Stoughton, 1899), p. 113.

3. See Michael Green, *Evangelism in the Early Church* (Grand Rapids: Wm. B. Eerdmans Publishing Co., 1970), p. 51.

4. See David L. McKenna, *The Jesus Model* (Waco, Texas: Word Books, 1977), esp. chapter 2, "Jesus, Our Model," pp. 169-179.

5. Related in slightly different form by Robert E. Coleman, *They Meet the Master* (Huntington Valley, Penn.: Christian Outreach, 1973), p. 143.

6. Commission on Evangelism, Report of a Commission on Evangelism Appointed by the Archbishops of Canterbury and York Pursuant to a Resolution of the Church General Assembly Passed at the Summer Session, 1943, *Towards the Conversion of England* (Westminister: The Press and Publications Board of the Church Assembly, 1945), p. 1.

8

Humor

Theme: Jesus used humor in his evangelism
Scripture Lesson: Psalm 2:4; Matthew 15:21-28

Introduction

When I was getting ready for my ordination to the gospel ministry in 1953, a senior deacon (now deceased) in my home church pulled me aside for a private conversation. The deacon had known me most of my life. He had taken a special interest in my welfare. I know he liked me because several times he had slipped me some money to help with my education. I was all ears.

You know what that senior deacon told me? He said, "Son, don't you ever laugh or smile or tell jokes in the pulpit. We had one pastor here," he continued, "who did all of those things, and we fired him."

I knew my well-meaning friend was telling the truth about firing one of our pastors. Uncertainty and doubt were my response to his advice about the use of humor. I am certain that, to some extent, his words have conditioned my use of humor throughout my ministry.

This idea that preachers should not tell jokes or make the congregation laugh is certainly not dead. A 1980 letter to the editor of a state Baptist paper said, "Neither do I appreciate preachers telling jokes from the pulpit to keep the congregation giggling."[1] While I can also appreciate a preacher who is more than a joker, I see essentially the same message here as I received from my senior deacon friend.

Contrary to all that you and I may have been taught about avoiding humor of any kind in public or private, a seventh principle of evangelism asserts that Jesus used humor in his evangelism. Likewise, if we pattern our evangelism after Jesus, we too will learn how to use humor in good taste and with proper grace.

God and Humor

Voltaire reportedly once said something to the effect that God is a comedian playing to an audience which is afraid to laugh! While the Scriptures do not picture God as a comedian, they do show him as one who laughs (see Ps. 37:13 for example).

Certainly the Book of Proverbs uses intentional humor. Some examples are: "A continual dripping on a rainy day and a contentious woman are alike" (Prov. 27:15); "The sluggard buries his hand in the dish, and will not even bring it back to his mouth" (Prov. 19:24); "Like a gold ring in a swine's snout is a beautiful woman without discretion" (Prov. 11:22).

"There seems to be laughter in creation itself," observed George Buttrick. Could a somber God have created a bullfrog or a giraffe? The small boy rightly exclaimed on his first sight of a camel, "I don't believe it."[2]

Jesus and Humor

Someone asked, "Did Jesus ever laugh?"

Another person answered, "I don't know, but he surely fixed me up to where I could!"

A letter reportedly written by Publius Lentulus to the Roman Senate in the days of Tiberius Caesar, described a man named Christ this way: "It cannot be remembered that any have seen Him laugh, but many have seen Him weep." Even if that letter is authentic, it contradicts the Christ of the New Testament.

The clearest examples of humor we have in the Bible are from Jesus. Think of the man swallowing a camel and straining out a gnat, or of the man with a big splinter in his own eye trying to take a speck of sawdust out of another's eye. Children are not attracted to somber persons, but they were attracted to Jesus. So, he must have been a joyful person who knew how to smile and laugh.

Even a four-year-old boy can see the humor of Jesus. Elton Trueblood's book on *The Humor of Christ* is dedicated "To Martin, who knew when to laugh." Four-year-old Martin was listening to his parents as they read from the Sermon on the Mount,

Why do you see the speck that is in your brother's eye, but do not notice the log that is in your own eye? Or how can you say to your brother, 'Let me take the speck out of your eye,' when there is a log in your own eye? You hypocrite, first take the log out of your own eye, and then you will see clearly to take the speck out of your brother's eye (Matt. 7:3-5).

Martin broke out laughing as Professor Trueblood read. Trueblood's first impulse was to think, *Why are you being so irreverent during family devotions?* However, he later realized that his son saw the humor in Christ's words. That was the genesis of his book.[3]

Admittedly, our biblical scholars have not made much of Jesus' use of humor until this century. Jakob Jonsson, in his pace-setting study on *Humor and Irony in the New Testament*, said the first scholar to his knowledge to make a special study of irony in the teaching of Jesus was Professor Henri Clavier in 1929 and 1930.[4]

Another problem which I suspect we have with the humor of Jesus is that we aren't sure just what is meant by his humor. Jonsson includes both humor and irony in his study because irony is one form of humor. Surely, humor has something to do with laughter or at least a smile. Humor in its truest sense is an expression of joy, sympathy, and optimism. It may be prophetic, educational, polemic, or just amusing. It may be expressed through such literary or rhetorical forms as wit, paradox, parables, allegory, and quid pro quo. Great humor is natural and spontaneous.[5]

Fundamental for both humor and irony is the sense of the comical. "Comedy deals with the absurd," says Kenneth Wolfe. "The very essence of the comic or of comedy is discrepancy. It is by the unmasking of discrepancy that comedy enables us to laugh."[6]

Perhaps a somewhat humorous incident in the life of the late Marshall McLuhan will illustrate for us this comical sense of the absurd. McLuhan was trying to charge a book in a New York store. "You're Marshall McLuhan, aren't you?" the clerk asked.

"Yes, thank you, not many people recognize me," McLuhan answered.

"I do, I've read every one of your books," the clerk said.

"You're flattering me," McLuhan said.

"I know, but I'll still need to see some identification," the clerk said.[7] Alas for the massive social and technological changes which threaten to smother us!

None of the foregoing is intended to play down the cross or the sense of sorrow in the life and ministry of Jesus. Jesus' humor was not humor for its own sake. His humor was educational and homiletic, "like the humour of the rabbis—it serves the purpose of enlightment, stimulation and joy, but, most of all, of illustrating religious truth."[8]

Examples of Humor in Evangelism

The case of the Canaanite woman whose daughter was demon possessed illustrates how Jesus used humor in his evangelism (see Matt. 15:21-28). Jesus was not insulting this lady by calling her a dog. Although the humor which is employed takes the form of irony, Clavier points out that the irony becomes milder because Jesus was not comparing her with the wild dogs, but the pet dogs who lived and ate inside the house. The diminutive form, *kunaria*, meaning a pet dog or a kind of puppy is the word used for dog.[9]

Probably, we should imagine that both of our Lord's initial words and the woman's responses were spoken with a twinkle in the eye. Jonsson comments on the dialogue in Matthew 15:24-27 as follows:

His statement that He is not sent but to the house of Israel and that the children's bread should not be cast to dogs is an ironical expression of the common view. The woman is clever enough to take up the discussion from the ironical point of view, as if she had said: "Very well, you are right. It is not your duty to help me, and I and my people are dogs from the orthodox point of view, but never mind all this. There should be something left for us anyhow, like when the little pet dogs get the crumbs from the master's table."[10]

Elton Trueblood was the first person to draw my attention to our Lord's use of humor in this case. "There is a more widespread recognition of this encounter as humorous than of any other particular part of the Gospel record," says Trueblood. "Thoughtful readers are more likely to recognize the humor here than at any other point."[11]

The case of Zacchaeus (Luke 19:1-10) is another example which reveals humor in evangelism. See the gentle humor when the little publican behaves like a boy. He does not hesitate to climb the sycamore tree. Very likely that looked somewhat comical to those present, but he didn't seem to care. What a sight![12]

Some other cases which show the use of Jesus' humor are: the case of the man who was carried by his four friends to Jesus (Mark 2:1-12), especially that part which relates to the scribes (Mark 2:6-11); the case of Simon the Pharisee (Luke 7:36-50), particularly the trap into which Simon fell (Luke 7:41-43); the case of the woman taken in the act of adultery (John 8:1-11), especially the irony involved in the statement: "Let him who is without sin among you be the first to throw a stone at her" (John 8:7); the case of Nicodemus (John 3:4; 10-12, esp.). the case of Nathanael (John 1:45-51); and the case of the woman at the well (John 4:11, esp.).[13]

More Implications of the Principle

Humorous anecdotes, stories, and parables do have a place in evangelism. However, such material must tell the truth, be in good taste, and should be sensitive to the feelings of everyone involved. It is always better to use humor at our expense than at someone else's.

Bailey Smith told a story at the 1974 Southern Baptist Pastor's Conference which illustrates how a pastor may use humor at his own expense. There was a young preacher who preached the truth but was having trouble with one critical parishioner especially. This fellow had as his favorite expression, "Great Day!" In business meeting or whereever, he would express himself, "Great Day!"

One Sunday morning the young prophet said as he arrived at the pulpit, "I'm preaching on the text, 'And Jesus fed five men with five thousand loaves of bread and two thousand fishes.' " The critical brother jumped up and said, "Great day, that's no miracle, I could do that!"

The young preacher was shattered and couldn't even preach his sermon. The next Sunday, out of spite, he announced correctly, "And Jesus fed five thousand men with five loaves and two fishes." He looked right down at the outspoken member and said, "And I guess you could do that too?"

"I certainly could," he said.

"How?" the preacher questioned.

"With what was left over from last Sunday," the man insisted.

An example of how not to use humor surfaced during the 1980 presidential campaign. A nationally known evangelist told an apocryphal story which violated good taste, was untrue, and insensitive. The evangelist reportedly claimed the story was an anecdote. He unwittingly brought pain and hurt to himself and to others by the misuse of humor.[14]

Some persons take us too literally in our evangelism. Especially is this true of children. When I was a pastor in Virginia, God gave us a remarkable revival one fall. I baptized more than forty persons at one service following that meeting. Many of the new converts were men. As I baptized each of them, I kept saying each time, "I baptize you my brother. . . ." That was too much for seven-year-old Robbie to take in. He turned to his mother and asked, "Mama, are all those men really Mr. Miles' brothers?"

A man was driving along in his car. Suddenly, he slammed on the brakes. His little boy fell down under the seat. His wife, over to the right, said, "Oh, you've killed him."

After a few moments the little boy climbed back up to the seat and said, "Mama, I'm not killed."

His mother said, "Shut up, yes you are!"

Fortunately, in real life things aren't always what we say they are. Unfortunately, in the practice of evangelism things aren't always what we say they are.

Humor will not only help us not to take others too literally but also it will prevent us from taking ourselves too seriously. Do you know how to laugh at yourself? I have had to learn.

Some years ago when we were living in Columbia, South Carolina, I was burning the candle at both ends. It had been a hectic week at the office. My doctoral dissertation on evangelism was in process. I drove my car across town to get one of those so-called, three-minue wash jobs which took thirty minutes. My mind was really not on what I was doing.

I drove back across town and pulled into the Exxon station where

I normally filled up with gas and told the attendant to fill it up. After a few minutes, the attendant said, "This thing is full already!"

It took seventeen cents to fill it up. I forgot that I had just filled it up as I got my car washed. You can imagine how foolish I felt. The only sensible thing I could do was laugh. I laughed at myself. The attendant laughed with me. When I told my family, they laughed too. That laughter helped relieve my tension.

Conclusion

"A smile is a curve that straightens out a lot of things." One thing people can do that animals can't is laugh! Although I think some animals appear to laugh.

Are you one of God's clowns? A popular song includes the question, "Where are the clowns?" The implication is that life is not worth living without those who can bring values into proper perspective with humor.

In a 1978 chapel address at The Southern Baptist Theological Seminary, Professor Bill J. Leonard spoke of "God's clowns." Leonard identified those men such as Noah, building an ark in the middle of the desert; or Simon Peter, claiming that we ought to obey God rather than man; or Martin Luther, presuming to challenge the authority of the establishment.

The roll call of such "clowns" is long. In Baptist history, it would include the familiar names of William Carey, Adoniram Judson, Luther Rice, L. R. Scarborough, C. E. Matthews, E. E. Autrey, and a great host of others.

If we practice the principle of humor in our evangelism, as did Jesus and our spiritual fathers, we shall also become God's clowns. Better it were that we should be clowns for Christ than to be the devil's fools.

When Jesus said, "Follow me, and I will make you fishers of men" (Matt. 4:19), do you know that he was using humor?[15] Especially do we see the humor when we compare that saying with the parallel in Luke 5:10. The phrase in Luke is "catching men," which literally means "taking men alive" or "capturing persons for life." Jesus is playfully using a term which had a bad meaning to convey his idea of making fishers of people out of fishers of fish. When we fish for people, we are engaging in a good kind of kidnapping!

Notes

1. *Baptist Courier,* Vol. 112, No. 33, Aug. 21, 1980, p. 4.

2. See George Arthur Buttrick, *Sermons Preached in a University Church* (New York: Abingdon Press, 1959), p. 52.

3. See Elton Trueblood, *The Humor of Christ* (New York: Harper & Row, Publishers, 1964), p. 9.

4. Jakob Jonsson, *Humor and Irony in the New Testament* (Reykjavik: Bokautgafa Menningarsjods, 1965), p. 11.

5. Ibid., pp. 16, 26-27.

6. This quotation is from an unpublished chapel message entitled "Christian Faith and the Comic," p. 2, given by professor Kenneth Wolfe to the Midwestern Baptist Theological Seminary, Kansas City, Missouri, in 1980. Jonsson also discusses the idea in *Humor and Irony in the New Testament,* p. 25.

7. See the editorial, "Marshall McLuhan," *The Kansas City Times,* Jan. 5, 1981, p. A-8.

8. Jonsson, p. 167.

9. Ibid., p. 178.

10. Ibid., p. 142.

11. Trueblood, p. 116.

12. See Jonsson, p. 163.

13. Ibid., pp. 178,179,200-207.

14. See the *Baptist Courier,* Vol. 112, No. 33, Aug. 21, 1980, p. 5.

15. See Jonsson, p. 140.

9
Balance

Theme: Jesus ministered to the whole person in a balanced way
Scripture Lesson: Hosea 7:8; Matthew 22:34-40

Introduction

Pablo Picasso died at the age of ninety-one. Often called the Michelangelo of the twentieth century, Picasso bequeathed to the world two hundred thousand works of art. Almost all critics agree that he was this century's foremost genius of modern art. "Picasso had more influence than any other artist in the history of the world," said British artist James Fitton, "he made people see in a different way."[1]

Jesus of Nazareth was the most influential evangelist in the history of the church. One of his enduring contributions is that he helps us to see in a different way. He is the Master Evangelist who enables us to see wholistically.

Jesus saw the whole person in relationship to his or her whole context and ministered to persons in a balanced way. That is the eighth principle which guided and guarded his evangelism.

I saw where a church in West Virginia advertised itself as "The Church with Acts 20:20 Vision." Have you looked at Acts 20:20 lately? The principle of balance asserts that Jesus had 20-20 vision, which resulted in his offering a whole gospel for the whole person in his or her whole context for the whole of time and eternity.

The Great Commission and the Great Commandment

The evangelism of Jesus was not like Ephraim, a half-baked cake, done on one side and raw on the other. He who gave us the Great Commission (see Matt. 28:16-20) also gave us the great commandment (see Matt. 22:37-40). As a matter of fact, they are found in the same Gospel.

The Great Commission says, "disciple all the nations," whereas the great commandment says in effect, "love God supremely and neighbor as self." These two are on a par with each other. Neither one supercedes or exhausts or explains the other.

Our Lord's evangelism was concerned with both outreach and inreach. It traversed both the outward journey and an inward one. His disciple-making was characterized by an inseperable interface between evangelism and ethics.

If we were to assume, as apparently some do, that the Great Commission symbolizes the evangelistic mandate and the great commandment the ethical mandate, we should see how intricately they are tied together in the life and ministry of the One who issued them both. What a strange imbalance we exhibit when we exalt either above the other. Jesus never did.

I believe it is a theological mistake to identify either the Great Commission or the great commandment exclusively with either evangelism or ethics. If we love God with our whole beings, we cannot help but share that consuming love with our lost neighbors. If we love our neighbors and they are hungry for the bread of life, we shall doubtlessly tell them about the Bread of life which we have found in Jesus Christ. That may be what Paul meant when he said, "the love of Christ controls us" (2 Cor. 5:14).

Then, too, one of the ways in which the Great Commission commands us to make disciples is by "teaching them to observe all that I have commanded you" (Matt. 28:20). Certainly, that would include what Jesus called "the great and first commandment" and the second commandment which is like the first (see Matt. 22:38-39). If all of the law and the prophets depend on these two commandments (see Matt. 22:40), we dare not ignore them in our disciple-making.

Therefore, our neighbor love cannot stop with the meeting of heart needs, body needs, or head needs. "Our neighbour is neither a bodyless soul that we should love only his soul," says John R. W. Stott, "nor a soulless body that we should care for its welfare alone;

nor even a body-soul isolated from society." Indeed, as Stott continues, "God created man, who is my neighbor, a body-soul-in-community. Therefore if we love our neighbor as God made him, we must inevitably be concerned for his total welfare—the good of his soul, his body, and his community."[2]

Charles H. Spurgeon caught this balance principle when he said, "A sinner has a heart as well as a head; a sinner has emotion as well as thoughts; and we must appeal to both."[3]

Before we leave these two "Greats" which our Lord gave to us, we might briefly ponder the beautiful internal balance which they exhibit, each in its own way. Consider first the great commandment. Our Lord teaches us to love God, neighbor, and self in a balanced way. Properly proportioned love involves the triangle of God, neighbor, and self.

Furthermore, our love for God is to be balanced with heart, soul, and mind (see Matt. 22:37). Mark 12:29, a parallel passage, adds that we are to love God with all our strength. The import of such admonition is that we are to love God with our total being: body, mind, heart, and soul, that is, with our whole personality. There is no part of us with which we are not to love God. Such balanced love rules out anti-emotionalism, anti-intellectualism, antinomianism, and Gnosticism. Is that the kind of balanced love which we are teaching our prospective disciples to have for God?

Moreover, the love which we are to extend to our neighbors is to be balanced by a healthy love for ourselves (see Matt. 22:39). I emphasize this point because it is possible for us to make so much of our death to self in the Christian life that we obliterate a proper and necessary self-image.

When Paul used the phrase, "Christ in you, the hope of glory" (Col. 1:27), I do not believe he was advocating the loss of our self-identity. We cannot love our neighbor in a balanced way unless we love ourselves in a balanced manner.

Do you make a place in your evangelism for such balanced love for self and neighbor? Or, do you see yourself as some worm crawling around on the earth?[4] My experience in evangelism has been that if I have a healthy self-image, the chances of my having a healthy image of others is enhanced.

While the balance in the Great Commission is not nearly so pronounced as that which we have been discussing in the great commandment, it is nevertheless a beautifully balanced command. If you will circle the three "alls" and the "always" in the text of the Revised Standard Version of Matthew 28:18-20, you will begin to see the sweet symmetry of this second "Great." See how the one who has *all* authority, commands us to disciple *all* nations, by teaching them to observe *all* that he commanded us, and then promises to be with us *always*. Those alls are very inclusive.

Now, notice the balance between the two ways through which we are to make disciples: "baptizing them . . . teaching them" (see Matt. 28:19-20). Those two participles in the Greek text are identical in case, number, gender, tense, and voice. One refers to a formal, liturgical ritual and drama; the other to a formal and informal educational activity which seeks to convey specific content, values, substance, and style.

I should also remind you of the internal balance in each of these two methods of making disicples. Our disciples are to be baptized in the name of the holy Trinity, that is, "the name of the Father and of the Son and of the Holy Spirit" (Matt. 28:19). We are to teach them to "observe all that" (Matt. 28:20) our risen Lord has commanded.

Again, let us ask ourselves if our evangelizing exhibits that kind of balance. Does our evangelism make room for all the "alls" of the Great Commission? Is our disciple-making characterized by both baptizing and teaching? Is our disciple-making trinitarian? Are we teaching our disciples to keep all of our Lord's commandments or only those which we happen to like best?

The Whole Person

Now, I should like to plunge forthrightly into an even more controversial area of our Lord's evangelism, namely his ministry to the whole person. Unfortunately, at this late date in church history we are still debating whether our Lord left us a soul gospel or a social gospel, as if the gospel could be chopped up like that.

When the paralytic, carried by four friends, was brought to Jesus through raising a rooftop, Jesus said to him, "My son, your sins are forgiven" (Mark 2:5). If Jesus had said first and only, "Rise, take up your pallet and walk" (see Mark 2:9,11), the scribes and other on-lookers would have never known he had the authority to forgive sins (see Mark 2:6-11). Jesus could have saved himself a lot of trouble simply by saying the right words, that is the words which the scribes wanted to hear.

I offer the case of the paralytic carried by four as an example that our Lord directed his evangelizing to the whole person. Whatever need was greatest at the moment, Jesus sought to meet it. While the paralytic had a physical problem, evidently he also had a sin problem. Our Lord dealt with both his spiritual and physical problems.

Such a balanced approach was characteristic of our Lord's evangelism. The Gerasene demoniac had problems with his mind, his body, his psyche, and his society (see Mark 5:1-20). Jesus helped him with every area of need. The official of Capernaum had problems with his son who was ill. Jesus healed the man's son. As a result, the official and "all his household" believed on Jesus (see John 4:46-54).

Jesus met persons at their points of need. He gave sight and light to the blind, acceptance and love to the outcasts, and food to the five thousand and to the four thousand.

He gave friendship to the friendless, "new wine" to the about-to-be-embarrassed bridegroom, and living water to the thirsty. He gave healing to the sick, freedom to the captives, power to the powerless, cleansing to the lepers, a listening ear to inquirers, good news to the poor, joy and laughter to the weeping, and forgiveness to all sinners who sought it.

That same Jesus, in his quiet and balanced way, still meets all persons at their points of need. That's where he met you and me.

A few years ago Doris Monroe told a group of Christian leaders that for every one thousand citizens in an average American community, about two of those are blind, two or three are deaf, and about thirty are mentally retarded.[5] We can be sure that our Lord expects us to meet each of these persons at his or her points of need.

Kenneth Chafin said on one occasion, "Evangelism moves forward best on the wings of ministry." When we, like Jesus, minister to the whole person in a balanced way, we shall literally see the truth of that statement and of this principle.

While living and working in South Carolina, I was deeply impressed by the ways Remount Baptist Church in Charleston ministered to the whole person. That church provided free transportation to Sunday worship services and to Sunday School. It offered graded worship services for children, geared to the age level of each child. It had a day-care program for children of working parents from 7:00 AM to 6:00 PM Monday through Friday. Kindergarten and weekday early education were provided for children, ages three, four, and five.

Other programs and services offered included: mother's day out on Fridays for mothers who needed a break from child care; Parents Without Partners for divorced, widowed, and separated; a fellowship to help single persons cope in a marriage-oriented society, meeting the last Tuesday of each month; regular jail services sharing the gospel with inmates of prisons; a Youth house, open every night of the weekend; an Alcoholics Anonymous chapter, using a church-owned building each Thursday evening and on Sunday afternoons; and special Christian education classes for mentally retarded children.

Remount Church, under the leadership of Pastor George Dye,[6] at one time had a goal of starting one new ministry each week. Such a balanced ministry to the whole person provides bridges into the lives of lost loved ones, friends, and associates. They offer an opportunity for web evangelism at its best.

Other Ramifications of Balance

If we imitate our Lord's evangelism and apply the prinicple of balance to our evangelism, we shall become as jealous for good deeds as we are for correct doctrine. One day while reading the Book of Titus for my daily devotions, I was struck by the phrase, "a people of his own who are zealous for good deeds" (Titus 2:14). Especially did that phrase "zealous for good deeds" stab me deeply.

At one point in my pilgrimage, I was far more zealous for correct doctrine than I was for good deeds. Even now I can easily generate a good head of steam for my favorite doctrines. But zeal for good works was not a major part of my tradition. Especially was that true in terms of understanding good deeds to involve what we now call Christian social action. The good deeds which I was taught to prize tended to be highly privatistic. Those public and corporate good deeds which were exhorted were primarily the safe ones, such as passing resolutions or signing petitions against Sunday movies, mixed bathing, licenses for the sale of alcoholic beverages, and so forth.

Alan Walker, the director of evangelism for the World Methodist Council, told South African Methodists, "There is no greater menace in the church than a born-again Christian without a social conscience." However, Walker also said, "But I am also convinced that the social activist Christian without a personal experience and commitment to Christ is as great a menace."[7]

While I should prefer not to draw that contrast so strongly, I do believe that a born-again soul doesn't necessarily mean a born-again mind. One's mind still needs to be renewed. Sanctification is a process which requires time and teaching.

If we apply the principle of balance in our evangelism, we shall balance our *going about* with our going about *doing good.* One said, "I know a man named Jesus who went about doing good. My concern is that I just go about." What about you? Are you going about doing good or just going about? If you are just going about, does it concern you? It should, for Jesus has given us an example that we should follow his steps.

Christianity is more deedology than it is creedology. We should endeavor to live our doctrine as well as talk about it. As a Hindu man said to missionary Otis Brady of Dominica, "That man walks and talks down the same road."

If we are balanced in our evangelism, we shall give attention to the welfare of both soul and body. One seminary student, a bodybuilder and a former "Mr. Kentucky," calls for balance between physical exercise and spiritual exercise. This student, who seeks to model that balance for youth, says, "You have to have a balance between taking care of yourself, having pride in your own abilities, and in realizing that God is most important."[8]

That call for balance surely fits in with the words of 3 John 2, "Beloved, I pray that all may go well with you and that you may be in health; I know that it is well with your soul." Some Christians give much attention to their souls and little or no attention to their bodies. Others give much attention to their bodies and little or no attention to their souls. What we all need is a balanced attention to both soul and body.

If we practice the principle of balance in evangelization, we shall balance our love for persons with our love for causes. Thomas Merton warns us of loving causes more than we love people. While I think some causes are so important that they must take precedence over the private welfare of one or a few persons, causes should generally exist to serve persons and to advance the welfare of humanity.

If we are balanced in our evangelism, we shall exhibit symmetry between our concern for "thereness" and "hereness." Adolph Hitler said, "We claim the earth, let the church have the beyond." No!

Jesus said, "You are the salt of the earth" (Matt. 5:13). Some Christians think they are just to be the salt of the church. The principle of balance calls for us to be the salt of the church and the salt of the earth.

The kingdom of God gives our evangelism the necessary vision of both the here and now and the there and then. I agree with Henry Drummond that during our Lord's earthly ministry the theme of the kingdom of God was never absent for a single hour from the thoughts of Jesus.[9]

If we are balanced in our evangelism, as was Jesus, we shall seek to reach both the down-and-out and the up-and-outs. Harold Begbie wrote a book entitled, *Twice-Born Men.*[10] It was about down-and-outs, persons on skid-row, who had been converted. We need to know about the power of God at work in that segment of society. But, more than that, in our time we need to see God at work converting the up-and-outs, the rich, the powerful, and the intellectuals.

If we follow Jesus in this principle of balance, we shall give attention to both *tact* and *contact* in our evangelism. I agree with Ernie Classen that tact and contact are two important points in witnessing. "The first is important," thinks Classen, "but not nearly as important as the second."[11] My contention is that, if we follow the principle of balance, we shall seek to maintain a healthy relationship between tact and contact.

Conclusion

One day I talked to a couple about their son who was doing social work. His degree was in sociology. They told me that their son was considering Christian counseling as a career. He had found a missing dimension in secular social work. The secular social scientist often cries out for a ministry to the total person.

I believe the quickest way to integrate one's personality is to get the individual soundly converted. To us who labor in evangelism is given the golden privilege of ministering to the whole person in a balanced way.

Notes

1. Quoted by *The State*, Columbia, S. C., April 9, 1973, p. 1-A.

2. See John Stott, "The Great Commandment . . . The Great Commission," *World Evangelization*, Information Bulletin No. 23, June, 1981, p. 5.

3. C. H. Spurgeon, *The Soul-Winner* (New York: Fleming H. Revell Co., 1895), p. 19.

4. It is good that they have revised that line in the hymn which used to say, "for such a worm as I." No human being, be he or she ever so vile and wretched is a mere worm crawling around on the earth.

5. Doris Monroe is a consultant in the Sunday School Department of the Sunday School Board of the Southern Baptist Convention who works with the mentally retarded.

6. Mr. Dye has now moved to another pastorate.

7. Quoted in *World Evangelization*, Information Bulletin No. 22, March, 1981, p. 10, a publication of the Lausanne Committee for World Evangelization.

8. See "Former 'Mr. Kentucky,' Now Seminarian, Has Uplifting Testimony," *The WORD and WAY,* Vol. 118, No. 1, Jan. 15, 1981, p. 4.

9. See Henry Drummond, *The New Evangelism* (London: Hodder and Stoughton, 1899), p. 91.

10. See Harold Begbie, *Twice-Born Men* (New York: Grosset & Dunlap, 1909).

11. Quoted by Ken Anderson, *A Coward's Guide to Witnessing* (Carol Stream, Ill.:, Creation House, 1972), pp. 138-139.

Epilogue
Retrospect and Prospect

Retrospect

We have examined eight master principles of evangelism: dignity, enfleshment, uniqueness, opportunism, sharing, dependency, humor, and balance. Five of these principles are partially summed up by the apostle Paul in what is perhaps the greatest single text on evangelism in the entire Bible, Colossians 4:5-6.

The principle of dignity, or respect for personality, may be caught up around the words: "Let your speech always be gracious, seasoned with salt" (Col. 4:6). The principle of enfleshment may be caught up around the words: "Conduct your selves wisely toward outsiders" (Col. 4:5). Outsiders is a technical term referring to those outside the Christian faith, those who are not members of the Christian household. So Paul admonished the Colossians to be careful about their lifestyle. A paraphrase might read: Watch the way you live toward outsiders because they are certainly watching you.

The principle of uniqueness may be caught up around the words: "so that you may know how you ought to answer every one" (Col. 4:6). Everyone is not asking the same question, so respect his or her God-given uniqueness.

The principle of opportunism may be caught up around the phrase: "making the most of the time" (Col. 4:5). Time is precious. Especially so because it is both seasonal and linear. One ought to use every moment of time as though he or she had to pay for it.

The phrase, "seasoned with salt" (Col. 4:6), is probably a reference to the use of humor in evangelization. Our speech is to be flavored and spiced with good, clean humor. Hence, Paul caught up the gist of the principle of humor in this text.

Regarding the principle of dependency, a word from Paul in Romans 1:4 yields a clue which may lead us to that principle: "designated Son of God in power according to the Spirit of holiness." William R. Newell said, "I have never seen a fully satisfactory explanation of the words" in that phrase.[1] John Knox tells us that many commentators see in these words a concession to the "adoptionist" Christology of the church at Rome. The best Knox can do with the exact phrase, "the Spirit of holiness," is to conclude: "No proposed explanation of its meaning is altogether satisfying."[2]

I believe this reference to the Spirit's role in the resurrection and exhaltation of Jesus reveals in a striking manner how the self-emptied Christ (see Phil. 2:7) was dependent upon the Holy Spirit. Moreover, that interpretation fits what is said about Christ offering himself without blemish to God "through the eternal Spirit" (Heb. 9:14).

As for the principle of sharing, I find it very educational that Paul, in references to the offering for the poor saints at Jerusalem, used the words *diakonia* (service), *koinonia* (fellowship), *eucharistia* (thanksgiving), *charis* (grace), and *dorea* (gift) to describe that collection (see 2 Cor. 9:1-15, esp. vv. 11-15). Paul, in other words, lifted their sharing with the poor saints in Jerusalem to the level of the Philippians' gifts to him: "a fragrant offering, a sacrifice acceptable and pleasing to God" (Phil. 4:18). It should not surprise us that Paul alone is credited with passing on to the church that saying of Jesus: "It is more blessed to give than to receive" (Acts 20:35). This "least of the apostles" was absolutely enamored with the principle of sharing.

Then, concerning the principle of balance, we need to cite only 1 Corinthians 9:22, "I have become all things to all men, that I might by all means save some." That same perfect proportion which we see in the great commandment and the Great Commission may also be seen here. Note the "alls": *all* things, *all* men, *all* means. If further evidence were needed, we might also point to Paul's great love hymn in 1 Corinthians 13. Paul seemed to be actually describing what Christ is like in 1 Corinthians 13:4-7.

Now, mind you, I do not contend for a moment that Paul self-consciously followed these master principles of evangelism as I have sought to spell them out. I am only suggesting that Paul sought to imitate Christ in his evangelism (see for example 1 Cor. 11:1), and that he wanted his converts to do likewise (see Phil. 2:1-11). I know of no man who knew the mind of Christ as did the apsotle Paul.

Prospect

These eight principles are by no means the only ones. While I consider them to be *master* and therefore *major* principles, there may well be other major and minor ones. Let me offer several additional possibilities on which I am now working.

Jesus intended to make disciples who would reproduce. That is the principle of *intentionality*. The Son of man came to seek and to save the lost (Luke 19:10). He who sent out the twelve and the seventy also sends us out today. He is more concerned about reproduction than production, multiplication than addition. One form of the Great Commission does have an imperative to disciple all nations. Even if there were no imperative command, the indicative of love would make God's wish tantamount to an imperative commandment.

Jesus intended to make some disciples; so did Paul; and so must we. One of the reasons we don't win more persons to Christ is that we don't intend to.

God is not in the cloning business. But he has put you and me in the business of spiritual reproduction. Our golden text might well be 2 Timothy 2:2, where four generations of witnesses are mentioned in one verse. Each of us is a link in that living chain of witnesses. "There is nothing optional about evangelism," said Professor Roy Fish. If this element of intentionality is present in our evangelism, we shall want to see the lost found and saved.

If just one Christian wins one unbeliever to Christ during one year and faithfully equips him or her and helps him or her catch a vision for reaching into all the world—and then if both of them do that for a second year, and four of them do it a third year—by the end of 10 years, the ministry of that first Christian will have expanded to 1,024 people. In only 10 more years 1,048,576 persons will have been touched if everyone remains faithfully committed to the task along the way. Then after a total of 32 years, 4.3 billion persons will have been affected.

Only through the process of reproduction can the gospel be heard throughout the whole world. Robert Coleman writes:

The test of any work of evangelism . . . is not what is seen at the moment, or in the Conference Report, but in the effectiveness with which the work continues in the next generation. Similarly the criteria upon which a Church should measure its success is not how many new names are added to the roll nor how much the budget is increased, but rather how many Christians are actively winning souls and training them to win multitudes.[3]

The late Carlyle Marney once asked: "What if God's redemption and God's purpose and God's coming and God's Kingdom are, insofar as their effective realization are concerned, in our hands? What if it is *unto us* that a child is born and a son is given?"[4]

You may have heard of John Vasser, a native of Poughkeepsie, New York. Vasser was a great disciple winner. He won people to Christ in homes, on streets, in the army, in hotel lobbies, on trains, and in almost every conceivable place and circumstance. Once he asked a lady in the lobby of a hotel, "Are you a Christian?" As Vassar listened to the woman's answer, her husband came down and interrupted the conversation.

Later, when her husband was told what had happened, he replied, "I suppose you told him it was none of his business."

"No," said the wife, "if you had heard him, you would have known that was indeed his business!"[5]

It was a master salesman who wrote, "Nothing happens unless we make it happen."[6] That may be a bit strong. But, I do believe that nothing very good happens in evangelism unless we intend it. Psalm 126:6-7 says, "He that goes forth weeping, bearing the seed for sowing, shall come home with shouts of joy, bringing his sheaves with him."

Is it possible that Jesus followed the principle of *receptivity* in his evangelism? "No one can come to me unless the Father who sent me draws him" (John 6:44). Nicodemus was receptive to Christ or he would not have sought him out and complimented him so highly. The two of John's disciples who followed Jesus were receptive to him or they would not have accepted his invitation to "Come and see" (John 1:39). The woman at the well was receptive to Jesus or she would not have said, "Sir, give me this water, that I may not thirst" (John 4:15). The Samaritans of Sychar were receptive to Jesus or they would not have "asked him to stay with them" (John 4:40). The official whose son was ill was receptive to Jesus, and that's the reason "he himself believed, and all his household" (John 4:53).

A certain Samaritan village refused to receive Jesus on one occasion. James and John were really put out, as is evidenced by their remark, "Lord, do you want us to bid fire come down from heaven and consume them?" (Luke 9:54). The sequel to that story says, "But he turned and rebuked them. And they went on to another village." (Luke 9:55-56).

Billy Graham told the Baptist World Alliance in 1980, "I'm finding a receptivity to the Gospel that I've never known in my ministry."[7] There does seem to be so many receptive unbelievers today in comparison with ten to twenty years ago.

One city in Kansas has gone to court to prevent the erection of a McDonald's restaurant. They did not succeed. Nevertheless, that McDonald's is quite different than the others you will see. It has no customary golden arches or brick exterior. Instead, there is an exterior of wood and stone. Its interior is finished in Williamsburg decor. All of that is to complement the architecture of the area.[8] Apparently, even restaurants have to adapt to their environment. How much more is such adaptation necessary in evangelization.

Could it be that there is a principle of *adaptation* in evangelism which arises out of the model of the incarnation of our Lord? And, if so, how does that differ, if indeed it does, from the principles of enfleshment and uniqueness?

One may see the principle of adaptation operating among today's Hare Krishnas. Members of that tiny sect, wore wigs on their shaved heads at the 1980 Kansas state fair in Hutchinson. The wig "allows us to relate to people in this culture more easily," said one of their spokesmen.[9]

Evangelistic methodology has to be adapted to the cultures in which it is used. Evangelism Explosion, for example, has learned that in Hong Kong a living room conversation is rare. It is better in Hong Kong to make an appointment at a nearby eating place than to call on persons in their homes. Callers in Australia may well wait until a second visit before beginning to talk seriously about spiritual matters. Illustrations with heavy military overtones may need to be replaced in West Germany, where two military defeats in this century have taken an understandable toll.[10]

A final possible principle which I lift up for future exploration is that of *self-revelation.*[11] This is the principle which asserts: Jesus revealed his true identity to others. Two biblical passages which may be used as launching pads are Exodus 3:13-15 and John 8:48-59.

One of the themes which stands out in John's Gospel is the self-revelation of Jesus as the Christ, the Messiah, the anointed One. You will remember that John is the Gospel which has the great "I am" sayings about Jesus: "I am the bread of life" (John 6:35); "I am the light of the world" (John 8:12); "I am the door" (John 10:9); "I am the resurrection and the life" (John 11:25); "I am the way, and the truth, and the life" (John 14:6). Jesus is revealing himself to us. He is telling us who he is.

Jesus, in John's Gospel, sought to make his true identity known to others in order that he might draw them to the Father. His self-revelation had an evangelistic purpose.

Almost every chapter of John's Gospel shows Jesus revealing his true identity to persons. In chapter 2, he reveals himself as the Giver of new wine. In chapter 3, he reveals himself as the Antidote for the poison of sin and as the Giver of eternal life. In John 4, he reveals himself as the Water of life. In John 5, he makes himself known as the Lord of the sabbath who forgives sin. In John 6, he reveals himself as the Bread of life. In John 7, he reveals himself as the Giver of the Holy Spirit, from whom would come rivers of living water. In John 8, he shows himself as the Light of the world and the great I AM.

God progressively makes himself known to us throughout the Bible. Jesus took the initiative in making himself known to us. If we are going to pattern our evangelism after Jesus, we too should reveal our true identity to others.

Paul said to "be imitators of God" (Eph. 5:1). The same apostle said, "Be imitators of me, as I am of Christ" (1 Cor. 11:1). So much of what we know about Paul, we learn from his own letters. He made his identity in Christ known. He did not hesitate to share autobiographically whenever he thought it was appropriate.

I know there is a quantum leap between who Jesus was and who we are. We should never forget the great distance between him and us. He was and is the unique Son of God. He was fully divine and fully human. And yet because he was the only perfect man, he is our model for revealing our true identity to others in order to evangelize them.

Moreover, we should be careful not to go around dumping our pearls before swine (see Matt. 7:6). There is such a thing as casting our precious things before wild boars, who will trample them and turn on us with their sharp tusks to rend us. Nevertheless, when we take off our masks and share the deep things of our spiritual pilgrimage with others, we speak with authority and with power.

Jesus made his true identity known in order to draw persons to the Father. If we share our Christian identity in order to point others to the Father, God will bless what we unveil and use it to touch some hearts and to tingle some minds.

Notes

1. William R. Newell, *Romans Verse by Verse* (Chicago: Moody Press, 1952), p. 6.

2. John Knox, *The Interpreter's Bible,* Vol. IX (New York: Abingdon-Cokesbury Press, 1954), pp. 382-384.

3. Robert E. Coleman, *The Master Plan of Evangelism* (Westwood, N. J.: Fleming H. Revell Co., 1963), p. 110.

4. Quoted by William H. Willimon in an Advent Meditation, "Unto Us," *The Christian Century,* XCVII, No. 42, Dec. 24, 1980, p. 1261.

5. Related by C. E. Autrey in *Messages on Evangelism* (Orlando, Fla.: The Golden Rule Press, 1962), p. 180.

6. Ernie Prichard, *Salesmanship for Christ* (Nashville: Broadman Press, 1972), p. 87.

7. See Leslie K. Tarr, "Billy Graham at the Baptist World Alliance," *Decision,* Nov., 1980 (Vol. 21, No. 11), p. 12.

8. See Judie Black, "McDonald's Opens Today Despite Foes," *The Kansas City Times,* September 8, 1980, p. B-3.

9. See Dick Haws, "Religious Groups Battle for Souls at Fair," *The Kansas City Times,* Sept. 8, 1980, p. B-2.

10. See "EE Presents Its Own 'State of the World,' " *EE Update,* Vol. 7, No. 10, October, 1980, pp. 1-2.

11. See Gaines S. Dobbins, *Evangelism According to Christ* (Nashville: Broadman Press, 1949), pp. 206-209. The term is used by Dobbins, but I am using it differently.